KU-498-022

Contents

Contributors

Katherine Ballard   Paediatric Macmillan Nurse, Birmingham Children's Hospital NHS Trust

Sharon Beardsmore Paediatric Macmillan Nurse, Birmingham Children's Hospital NHS Trust

Moira Bradwell   Paediatric Macmillan Nurse, Birmingham Children's Hospital NHS Trust

Carol Chenery   Formerly Paediatric Macmillan Nurse, Birmingham Children's Hospital NHS Trust

Carol Davies   Paediatric Macmillan Nurse, Birmingham Children's Hospital NHS Trust

Nicki Fitzmaurice   Paediatric Macmillan Nurse, Birmingham Children's Hospital NHS Trust

Sue Neilson   Paediatric Macmillan Nurse, Birmingham Children's Hospital NHS Trust

Acknowledgements

This book could not have been completed without help and support from the following colleagues:

Nigel Ballantine
Faith Gibson
Joy Hall
Kath Hill
Helen Langton
Sue Woodhouse

Foreword

Practitioners in paediatric palliative care are only too aware that the evidence base for their practice remains limited at the current time. This leaves practitioners heavily reliant on anecdotal evidence based on their own or a colleague's experience and the knowledge of the child's parents. On its own, this evidence is, of course, extremely valuable, as demonstrated by the success of its application in the 25% of children and young people in the UK who die as a result of their cancer. It is towards the care of these children, young people and their families that this book is aimed.

'Learning on the job' remains the most popular route to expert practice in this specialist area of children's nursing. There are few educational programmes available, which means that, where they do exist, places on courses are limited, with geographical distance preventing many from participating. For those who have already reached the level of expert, the education available may not be what they require. Both the novice and the expert nurse are required to evidence their practice by reference to published research findings. This book is a valuable resource that will guide practitioners in their decision-making, facilitating the delivery of safe, effective and individualised family-centred care by specialist and non-specialist nurses.

What is particularly exciting about this book is that it brings together the shared expertise of a group of experienced nurses working in the real world of practice. Through their collaborative efforts they demonstrate the complexities of supporting children, young people and their families through the palliative phase of their illness. They have examined their role closely and have been prepared to share their personal knowledge. They have critically examined their repertoire of paradigm cases and, fortunately for the reader, have presented many of these real clinical situations as evidence, bringing together aspects of research and practical knowledge.

Dealing with the needs of dying children and their families can promote stress and anxiety in healthcare professionals — wanting to 'get it right', feeling threatened by a lack of specialist knowledge and skills and by personal fears and feelings. This book addresses all these areas with sensitivity and illustrates how important it is for families to be supported by healthcare professionals at every stage of their palliation journey. It is this relationship that is striking throughout the book. Readers will be guided in their practice towards developing professional relationships with families that embody true partnership. Maintaining quality of life, delivering individualised symptom-focused care and supporting the family at the time of death remain the primary goals.

This book echoes these goals and presents a point in time in the care of children dying from malignant disease. It is hoped that, as well as answering many questions and facilitating expert practice, this book will challenge readers to seek to further their evidence base through child- and family-focused research.

Faith Gibson, PhD, MSc (Cancer Nursing),
RSCN, RGN, ONC Cert, Cert Ed, RNT
Lecturer in Children's Nursing Research
Great Ormond Street Hospital for Children NHS Trust

Introduction

This book aims to provide an overview of the care given to children in the palliative phase of their malignant disease. It comprises the theoretical components of palliative care, linked to the practical experience of the West Midlands Paediatric Macmillan Team (WMPMT). The book presents a number of case studies to illustrate specific points within the text. Relevant management strategies, together with theoretical frameworks, are discussed. Concepts of paediatric palliative care and the role of the team will be introduced here and expanded on in subsequent chapters.

Palliative care is defined by the World Health Organization (1998) as:

> *'The active total care of patients whose disease is not responsive*
> *to curative treatment. Control of pain, of other symptoms and*
> *psychological, social and spiritual problems is paramount. The goal*
> *of palliative care is achievement of the best quality of life for patients*
> *and families.'*

Paediatric palliative care may be needed for a wide range of conditions, which differ from adult diseases. At least 10 in 10,000 children between 0 and 19 years of age require palliative care, giving a total of at least 15,000 children requiring palliative care in the UK at any one time (National Council for Hospice and Specialist Palliative Care Services, Association for Children with Life-Threatening or Terminal Conditions and their Families [ACT] and Association of Children's Hospices, 2001).

In 1997, ACT and the Royal College of Paediatrics and Child Health (ACT/ RCPCH, 1997) identified four broad groups of children likely to require palliative care:

- potentially curable, but treatment may fail (life threatening), eg. cancer
- premature death possible, but long periods of normal life, eg. cystic fibrosis, muscular dystrophy
- slowly progressive, eg. Batten's disease
- life limiting, not progressive, but vulnerability and complications likely to cause premature death, eg. cerebral palsy.

Within these four groups, palliative care may be required from infancy and continue over many years, while others may not need it until they are older and then only for a short period of time (Goldman, 1998).

The main goals of curative treatment are to cure disease and prolong life. The move to palliative care involves a change in philosophy, where prolonging life is no longer the primary aim, the focus being the quality of the life remaining. The aim of palliative care, therefore, is to maintain as much normality for the family as possible and to achieve the best quality of life for the child. Care should follow the child from one clinical environment to another, depending on individual need. In order for this to be achieved, appropriate expertise in the management of physical symptoms must be available, together with psychological support for both the child and family.

Birmingham Children's Hospital is one of the largest regional centres for paediatric oncology and haematology in the UK, with approximately 160–170 newly diagnosed patients a year under the age of 16 years (Curry, 2003). The West Midlands is an area of ethnic and cultural diversity. From 1997 to 2002, approximately 19% of patients diagnosed with cancer were non-Caucasian (Parkes, 2002). The specific needs and values of such ethnically diverse groups must be considered when care is delivered, and must involve individual assessment of need.

Survival rates from the National Registry of Childhood Tumours (NRCT, 1996) show that in the most recent period, with complete follow-up, 73% of all children with cancer survived five years, leaving 27% who died from their disease within five years. In the West Midlands, from 1998 to 2002, an average of forty-two childhood deaths a year occurred as a consequence of cancer (Curry, 2003).

The WMPMT was established at Birmingham Children's Hospital in 1992 and currently consists of five whole-time equivalent clinical nurse specialists. Family-centred care is offered at all stages of the child's illness – from diagnosis, during treatment, at the time of relapse, and during the palliative and bereavement phases. The philosophy of the team, at all stages of care, focuses on the physical and psychosocial support of the child and family and liaison with community staff.

The WMPMT aims to develop relationships with the child and family and the primary health care team at the point of diagnosis. Disseminating knowledge and skills within the community and working closely with GPs, district nurses and the multidisciplinary team ensure the delivery of local, quality care. Primary health care teams are empowered to act as carers. The role of the team is primarily an advisory and coordinating role. A key feature of this is the ability to liaise with the wide variety of staff involved in the child's care, facilitating the communication process and ensuring widespread liaison. The number of professionals involved in palliative care varies, depending on the needs of the child and family. Appreciating and understanding each professional's role enables a better partnership in care. Adopting a flexible and responsive approach allows the individual needs of the child and family to be met. As coordinators of care, the team ensures that lines of communication are kept open and that disciplines work together to provide optimum care.

It is hoped that the team's experience will add to the book and provide an interesting and stimulating read for professionals wishing to increase their knowledge on this subject.

References

ACT/RCPCH (1997) *A Guide to the Development of Children's Palliative Care Services*. ACT/RCPCH, London

Curry H (2003) Oncology Data Manager, Birmingham Children's Hospital

Goldman A (1998) ABC of palliative care: special problems of children. *BMJ* **316**: 49-52

National Council for Hospice and Specialist Palliative Care Services, ACT and Association of Children's Hospices (2001) *Joint Briefing: Palliative Care for Children*. Number 1

NRCT (1996) Population-based survival rates for children aged under 15 years in Great Britain. Oxford

Parkes S (2002) Tumour Registry. Birmingham Children's Hospital

World Health Organization (1998) *Cancer Pain Relief and Palliative Care in Children*. WHO, Geneva

Disclaimer

The West Midlands Paediatric Macmillan Team's experience and practice are outlined in this book.

The information documented in *Chapter 5, Section D*, is taken from the guidelines produced by the Departments of Haematology, Oncology and Pharmacy at Birmingham Children's Hospital NHS Trust.

While much care has been taken to ensure that the information quoted is accurate, it has itself been collated from a variety of sources. In common with the philosophy of other sections of this book, the information is provided to inform the reader regarding practice at Birmingham Children's Hospital. It should be understood that few drugs are licensed for symptom control in palliative care, and, in consequence, practice between different centres may vary considerably.

The reader's attention is drawn to the fact that many drugs or doses in the tables in *Section D* are licensed for the indication quoted. In order to deliver the treatment it may also be necessary to administer licensed preparations in unlicensed ways and/or by unlicensed routes. In some cases the information relates to the use of unlicensed 'Specials' preparations.

Neither the authors, the publishers, Birmingham Children's Hospital NHS Trust nor Macmillan Cancer Relief accept any liability arising from the use or misuse of the information on drug treatment or wider practice documented herein.

1

The journey to palliative care

Despite improved treatment strategies in paediatric oncology, approximately a quarter of patients in the United Kingdom still die as a result of their disease (National Registry of Childhood Tumours, 1996). Once it is apparent that cure is no longer possible, the focus becomes the relief of symptoms (Stevens, 1995; Committee on Bioethics and Committee on Hospital Care, 2000), with the emphasis of treatment changing from curative to palliative.

The move to palliative care, however, is frequently ill defined. Many issues can present obstacles to the application of a palliative care model (Hicks and Lavender, 2001; Hilden *et al*, 2001). Rather than a discernible shift of emphasis, there is an evolving change. Potential 'grey areas' during this transition can create debate and difficulties in management.

This chapter will discuss these issues for the child, family and professionals. Consideration will be given to the shifting emphasis of care and factors that influence decisions on the journey. Several themes, including communication, siblings, and paediatric oncology outreach nurses, will be introduced in this chapter and explored in depth elsewhere in the text.

Starting the journey

For a family, the news that cure is no longer possible is devastating. Uncertainty about the future, which pervades treatment and follow-up (Lansdown and Goldman, 1988), is replaced by loss of hope and combinations of emotions including grief, trepidation and disbelief (Stevens, 1995).

When a family is informed that their child is no longer curable, the emotional nature of the discussion can impair their ability to hear and absorb information. It is, however, important that the message is clear. In an attempt to protect the child and family, professionals may disguise information in subtlety. A consequence of this subtlety may be that the message becomes ambiguous. It is therefore important to confirm understanding during and subsequent to the discussion. Moreover, if further palliative therapy is offered, the nature of the intervention should be reinforced. These initial discussions should be well documented, as it is common for decisions taken at these times to be questioned later.

Ideally, the relationship developed with the professional care team during earlier phases of treatment will engender trust in this new and formidable situation. The family are then likely to feel confident that they can verbalise their thoughts, clarify information and pursue questions. The information that the doctor communicates should be delivered in a style that the child and family will understand. Furthermore, all options must be presented and given due consideration. Parents report that the information and recommendations given by professionals are the most significant influences in their decision-making (Hinds *et al*, 1997). However, the manner in which information is presented to a family can significantly influence their decisions, and the suggestion that treatment is possible can potentially encourage misplaced hope (Koedoot and de Haes, 1995). Moreover, relationships of power can have an impact on the decisions made by the child and family, as can the way in which options are presented to them. For example, if professionals give treatment modalities precedence over palliation, the family are more likely to choose the former.

Following the initial discussion, parents will often find themselves as messengers, having to relay the thoughts of the doctor and plan of action to family and friends. This, in turn, is likely to prompt questioning from the wider family that the parents may feel unable to deal with. Having a witness present at discussions (eg. the paediatric Macmillan nurse) can provide a mechanism for reviewing information. The opportunity to repeat consultations should be available, and be offered to the family.

With the advent of the internet it is possible for families to readily obtain information regarding treatments internationally (Hicks and Lavender, 2001). Even if parents choose not to access additional information, well-meaning friends or relatives frequently do so on their behalf. In consequence, families may present data regarding innovative treatments that are available globally. While it can be difficult to review these candidly, when it is clear to the professional team that cure is not possible, such initiatives should be greeted with respect and compassion. Experience indicates that failure to do so may create barriers in palliative care.

Increasingly, families ask for second opinions from other centres. For many families this represents verification of the information already received from the child's treatment centre. They merely need assurance that everything possible has been done, in order to cope (Vickers and Carlisle, 2000). For some, however, this represents a continuing search for alternative treatment options. While most families will search with the knowledge that any potential treatment will be, at most, an attempt to extend life, for a small number this will reflect ongoing pursuit of curative therapy. Some may wish to pursue treatment options that offer no realistic chance of cure, while also being toxic and impractical. Although in principle it is possible to balance ongoing treatment and symptom management, it may be impossible to steer such families towards palliation and thus good symptom relief.

Communication

Good communication between the child, family and professionals is essential in the palliative phase of disease. Open communication is considered most effective (Kruijver *et al,* 2000), with the child and family participating as fully as possible in decision-making (Stevens, 1995). This will enable the child, family and professionals to negotiate care. The pattern should have been set at diagnosis (Masera *et al*, 1999) and maintained throughout treatment.

It is considered best practice in paediatric oncology for the child to participate as fully as possible in decision-making (Committee on Bioethics and Committee on Hospital Care, 2000). Such participation, however, requires the child to be cognisant with his/her disease status. Adults frequently underestimate children's awareness and understanding (Peace, 1994). Children almost always know more than adults think they do (Goldman, 1998). Children with cancer can have a better understanding of:

- their disease than adult cancer patients (Peace, 1994)
- the irrevocability of death than their peer group (Clunies-Ross and Lansdown, 1988).

This gives them the ability to be involved in decision-making, and the capacity to deal with the knowledge of their impending death (Nitschke *et al*, 1982).

Children need to receive accurate, age-appropriate information in clear language and at a pace that they control (Hicks and Lavender, 2001). Younger children, for example, will require simple explanations and exploration through play. Older children may need the opportunity to spend time alone with medical or nursing staff, to allow deeper questioning and discussion. An environment where a child is able to express worries and concerns is consequently invaluable (Vickers and Carlisle, 2000).

Parents may fear that being honest with their child about the prognosis may result in him/her 'giving up'. Giving a child appropriate explanations is more likely to alleviate anxiety than instil it (Peace, 1994), and allowing a child to talk openly can promote feelings of control and choice (see *Chapter 4*).

Belief systems

It is important that professionals are sensitive to how family members make sense of their lives and the situation they find themselves in (Kavanagh, 1994). For some this is based around a religious belief; for others there is less formal structure to what gives their life meaning, purpose and fulfilment. Cultural customs and expectations about illness, dying, death and mourning will also vary (Stevens, 1995). Moreover, the depth of communication with families may be influenced by cultural practices and beliefs (Bruera and Sweeney, 2002). Dying children and their families will have a wide range of personal and family values, spanning diverse groups culturally, ethnically and linguistically (Hicks and Lavender, 2001). It is therefore essential that professionals have an appreciation of a family's culture, religion and beliefs, in order to meet their needs (Nyatanga, 1997).

A parent or child's previous experience of death can also have a significant impact on their wishes in the transition to palliative care. Families may recount stories of relatives or friends who have died and whom they perceive to have suffered difficult or distressing symptoms or management. Likewise, the child and family may have experienced other children dying from disease or treatment-related causes. Their perception of events, good or bad, can influence their views and decisions regarding their own situation. Listening is crucial in order to pick up cues about how families perceive the experience of death, and thereby negotiate an appropriate way forward (Kavanagh, 1994).

Just as a family's belief system will influence decision-making, so will those of the professional team. It is therefore essential that those involved in the care of children with life-threatening illness consider and reflect upon the issues that may influence their own decision-making (see *Case study 1.1*).

Case study 1.1

Joe, aged ten years, had glioblastoma multiforme. He had received conventional treatment with radiotherapy. The family understood from the outset that Joe's prognosis was very poor. He now had disease progression and was symptomatic. The oncologist saw the family in clinic jointly with one of the nurses. He informed the family that Joe's tumour was progressing, and suggested further treatment with chemotherapy. Joe was told that his tumour was 'playing up' and that he needed some different treatment. Joe's parents talked of wanting to enjoy as much of the time that they had got left, at home, together with Joe. Nevertheless, they expressed great faith in their doctor and said that they were willing to be advised by him.

Key considerations

Ideally, the doctor and multidisciplinary team in this case study would have taken into account all the influencing factors before suggesting more treatment. The factors that need to be considered by Joe, his parents and the professional team include:

- how toxic will the chemotherapy be?
- will the administration and side-effects of treatment necessitate periods in hospital?
- will the treatment afford the family quality time with their child?

In this case study, the family have specifically stated that they wished to be at home, and their language suggested a desire that treatment would not detract from this. They appear to understand that they have limited time left with their son. The oncologist and multidisciplinary team appear not to have acknowledged the family's requests.

Doctors have been reported as finding imparting bad news particularly stressful, and describe feeling powerless and guilty about being unable to achieve a cure (Koedoot and de Haes, 1995; Hilden *et al*, 2001). In consequence they may continue to give treatment in order to avoid such painful issues. Research has shown that paediatric oncologists frequently recommend continued treatment for patients despite repeated relapses (Hilden *et al*, 2001). This may reflect the personal difficulties that physicians themselves incur when moving from active treatment into the palliative arena (Wolfe, 2000). Clearly, it is demanding to communicate such distressing information to a family. Families are likely to be emotional and may find it hard to articulate their feelings. In these circumstances it is easy to suggest further interventions in an attempt to soften the impact and minimise distress for all parties.

Oncology nurses are less likely than physicians to support further treatment (Damrosch *et al*, 1993) and may consequently be guilty of influencing discussions and steering families away from further interventions. If nurses adopt a passive role, however, there is no debate and the physician's views remain unchallenged. It has been suggested that when nurses request collaboration in decision-making, the intent is to influence the decision not to collaborate (Jenks, 1993). Nevertheless, collaboration is essential in the transition to palliative care. Multidisciplinary debate should be routine practice, providing a forum for each member of the team to challenge assumptions and clinical opinions.

There are unequivocal benefits to be gained from a nurse representative being present at consultations. The nurse is able to reiterate the content of the medical discussion both immediately and in future contact with the family. It is also likely that merely by being present the nurse will provide support for both the physician and the family.

Changes in treatment protocols

Despite substantial improvements in survival rates for childhood cancer, for some groups of patients the prognosis remains poor. A culture of more intensive therapy has developed, particularly for patients with a poor prognosis, in an attempt to improve survival (Dunkel *et al*, 1998). Increasingly, treatment options beyond first-line management are being used in an attempt to rescue patients.

Some children and families may experience difficulty in reconciling themselves to the option of no further treatment. For them the opportunity to have palliative chemotherapy, radiotherapy or taking part in a phase I/II trial (*Chapter 3*) may be considered a means of 'buying time' and giving hope (Stevens *et al*, 2004, unpublished). It is essential that the benefits of such an undertaking are measured against the inherent discomfort or harm that may be incurred (Ackerman, 1995). There may, however, be circumstances when palliative radiotherapy or chemotherapy provides the best symptomatic management (*Chapter 3*).

Supportive care

Clinic/hospital attendance

In the West Midlands Region, children who are in the palliative phase of their disease, and their families, are not generally given routine follow-up appointments in the oncology clinic. They are encouraged to make appointments as necessary in an attempt to limit trips to the regional centre where they are unlikely to hear any new information. Such an 'open-door policy' enables review of decisions, preventing feelings of abandonment and facilitating acceptance (Stevens, 1995). Some families will wish to persevere with regular clinic visits, and should, of course, continue to do so while the child remains well enough. For others, sitting in the waiting area of a busy treatment clinic can be intensely painful when they are aware that their child is not curable.

Full blood counts and blood and platelet support

During treatment, children are commonly supported with blood products based upon changes in the blood count. Families become accustomed to this mode of monitoring, and derive comfort from the knowledge that such routine examination will detect a fall in platelets or haemoglobin before problems arise. In the palliative phase of disease it is considered ideal to treat children with blood products based upon symptomatology, the intent being to maximise their quality of life with least intervention (Beardsmore and Alder, 1994). It is therefore suggested that blood counts are taken only in response to deterioration of symptoms. Clearly, such changes in management can lead to much anxiety.

Nevertheless, it is prudent to discuss and agree a plan with the family, early in the palliative phase, regarding the monitoring of blood counts and the use of blood products (*Chapter 5, Section B*).

Treatment of infections

During treatment there are very specific guidelines for parents and professionals about the early diagnosis and treatment of infections with intravenous antibiotics. In the palliative phase of disease, however, the emphasis shifts away from intervention. Consequently, infections are often managed with oral antibiotics or not treated at all. Frank discussion and negotiation with the family early in the palliative phase is invaluable and can prevent misunderstanding later. For those children who have recently discontinued treatment or have been receiving palliative chemotherapy, it can be particularly difficult to move family and professionals away from administration of intravenous antibiotics.

The ability of a patient to take oral medication will clearly influence whether or not to give oral antibiotics. As disease progresses, the child may be unable or unwilling to take medication orally. Furthermore, the influence of antibiotics on the infection may be limited. There is, however, a reasonable argument for treating infections with unpleasant symptoms, such as urinary tract infection, even in patients who are very unwell.

Deciding how to respond to pyrexia can be particularly difficult in a child who may have disease-driven fever. Candid discussion with the families of children who have disease processes where this is prevalent can enable strategies to be put in place early and prevent misunderstanding later. Strategies may include:

- treatment with antipyretics
- tepid sponging
- intervention with antibiotics only with a proven or obvious focus of infection.

Home care

If further treatment is not undertaken, it is important to discuss where the child is to be cared for. The majority of families will wish to care for their dying child at home (Vickers and Carlisle, 2000). Paediatric oncology outreach nursing posts were developed in the UK in the 1980s in response to a belief in choice for families, and to enable those who wished to care for their child at home to do so with the support of experts in paediatric palliation (*Chapter 2*).

Maintaining normality

The sick child should have the opportunity to continue to attend school. School represents their normal pattern of activity and provides a link with peers (Goldman, 1998). It also provides structure to the day, which most children find comforting. Bouffet and colleagues' (1997) study revealed that 60% of palliative oncology children wished to continue to attend school until the late stages of their disease, with poorly controlled symptoms being cited as the reason why the majority of the remainder failed to do so. Continued school attendance can, nevertheless, engender feelings of concern for both parents and school staff. A school visit to provide information and answer queries can increase the confidence of the child, family and staff.

Although it is difficult for parents to continue their normal pattern of discipline with their dying child, it is recommended. Discipline provides a framework and security for children (Foye and Sulkes, 1994). Likewise, over-indulging the sick child with treats and special favours can create problems (Thomas, 1994). Failure to maintain the norm may result in the child feeling fearful and vulnerable (Harding, 2000). Siblings may also perceive that the sick child is being treated in a special way and feel resentful.

Maintaining hope

Decisions at this stage of the disease process are particularly difficult because of the need to confront the prospect of death and the loss of hope (Koedoot and de Haes, 1995). There are, nevertheless, ways to promote and maintain hope other than with treatment options. The challenge for the palliative care worker is to encourage patients and families to seek hope-fostering strategies (Ahmedzai, 1994). The specialist practitioner will encourage the child and family to consider what is important to them, to set goals that are attainable and within a realistic time frame (Kruijver *et al*, 2000). Short-term goals are particularly important when working with young children (Goldman, 1998), whose perception of time is limited. The aim may be a special trip, holiday or merely a significant date, eg. a birthday, a wedding or Christmas day.

There are a number of foundations that grant wishes for sick children, and in some cases their families. Although travel wishes may be unrealistic in the latter stages of disease, such foundations are extremely successful at securing a variety of other options, including obtaining an item such as a computer, arranging attendance at an event such as a concert or football match, or even meeting a celebrity. Once a goal is near or reached, it can be helpful to set further goals in order to maintain hope (see *Appendix 1* for list of Wish Foundations).

Length of palliative phase

The median period of palliation in paediatric oncology has been quoted as 6 weeks (Goldman and Bowman, 1990); however, in the West Midlands Paediatric Macmillan Team's experience, this time frame is not helpful in practical terms, owing to the wide range of duration (1 day to 18 months). The palliative phase may be prolonged and can consequently require long-term commitment from the multidisciplinary team.

Summary

Whatever the journey into palliation entails, it is clearly a distressing time for the family and can prove difficult for the multidisciplinary team as they negotiate the way forward. For some children the transition period is short and well defined, but for others it may be prolonged, tenuous and encompass trials of experimental therapy (Stevens *et al*, 2004, unpublished). Precise guidelines for the transition to palliative care do not exist. The values and principles of the child, family and professionals – personal, cultural and philosophical – will all influence the way forward (Masera *et al*, 1999; Schonholzer, 1999). Families will need the team to be honest and supportive, and to advocate on their behalf throughout this journey. The strength of the continuing relationships with the family will be reflected in the success of the transition (Stevens, 1995).

References

Ackerman TF (1995) Phase 1 pediatric oncology trials. *J Pediatr Oncol Nurs* **12**(3): 143–5

Ahmedzai S (1994) Suffering and the art of compassion and hope (Editorial). *Progress in Palliative Care* **2**(6): 217–21

Beardsmore S, Alder S (1994) Terminal care at home — the practical issues. In: Hill L (Ed). *Caring for Dying Children and their Families*. Chapman and Hall, London: 162–76

Bouffet E, Zucchinelli V, Costanzo P, Blanchard P (1997) Schooling as part of palliative care in paediatric oncology. *Palliat Med* **11**(2): 133–9

Bruera E, Sweeney C (2002) Palliative care models: international perspective. *J Palliat Med* **5**(2): 319–27

Clunies-Ross C, Lansdown R (1988) Concepts of death, illness and isolation found in children with leukaemia. *Child Care Health Dev* **14**(6): 373–86

Committee on Bioethics and Committee on Hospital Care (2000) Palliative care for children. *Pediatrics* **106**(2 Pt 1): 351–7

Damrosch S, Denicoff AM, St Germain D *et al* (1993) Oncology nurse and physician attitudes toward aggressive cancer treatment. *Cancer Nurs* **16**(2): 107–12

Dunkel IJ, Garvin JH, Goldman S *et al* (1998) High dose chemotherapy with autologous bone marrow rescue for children with diffuse pontine brain stem tumors. *J Neurooncol* **37**: 67–73

Foye HR Jr, Sulkes SB (1994) Developmental and behavioral pediatrics. In: Behrman RE, Kliegman RM (Eds). *Nelson Essentials of Pediatrics*. 2nd edn. WB Saunders, Philadelphia: 1–54

Goldman A (1998) ABC of palliative care: special problems of children. *Br Med J* **316**: 49–52

Goldman A, Bowman A (1990) The role of oral controlled-release morphine for pain relief in children with cancer. *Palliat Med* **4**: 279–85

Harding R (2000) The impact of diagnosis. In: Langton H (Ed). *The Child with Cancer: Family-centered care in practice*. Baillière Tindall, Harcourt Publishers, London: 37–78

Hicks MD, Lavender R (2001) Psychosocial practice trends in pediatric oncology. *J Pediatr Oncol Nurs* **18**(4): 143–53

Hilden JM, Emanuel EJ, Fairclough DL *et al* (2001) Attitudes and practices among pediatric oncologists regarding end-of-life care: results of the 1998 American Society of Clinical Oncology Survey. *J Clin Oncol* **19**(1): 205–12

Hinds PS, Oakes L, Furman W *et al* (1997) Decision making by parents and healthcare professionals when considering continued care for pediatric patients with cancer. *Oncol Nurs Forum* **24**(9): 1523–8

Jenks JM (1993) The pattern of personal knowing in nurse clinical decision making. *J Nurse Educ* **32**(9): 399–405

Kavanagh M (1994) Spiritual care. In: Hill L (Ed). *Caring for Dying Children and their Families*. Chapman and Hall, London: 106–22

Koedoot N, de Haes JCJM (1995) Deciding to cease active cancer treatment: issues in process and outcome. *Progress in Palliative Careb* **3**(2): 45–52

Kruijver IPM, Kerkstra A, Bensing JM, van de Wiel HB (2000) Nurse-patient communication in cancer care. A review of the literature. *Cancer Nurs* **23**(1): 20–31

Lansdown R, Goldman A (1988) The psychological care of children with malignant disease. *J Child Psychol Psychiatry* **29**(5): 555–67

Masera G, Spinetta JJ, Janovic M *et al* (1999) Guidelines for assistance to terminally ill children with cancer: a report of the SIOP working committee on psychosocial issues in pediatric oncology. *Med Pediatr Oncol* **32**: 42–8

National Registry of Childhood Tumours (1996) *Population-based Survival Rates for Children Aged under 15 Years in Great Britain*. Oxford

Nitschke R, Sexaver CL, Wunder S (1982) Therapeautic choices made by patients in end stage cancer: *Behavioural Paediatrics* **101**(3): 471–6

Nyatanga B (1997) Cultural issues in palliative care. *Int J Palliat Nurs* **3**(4): 203–8

Peace G (1994) Children and advocacy: issues in palliative care. *Bulletin* **9**(June): 4, 8. Trent Palliative Care Centre, Sheffield

Schonholzer M (1999) Comment on: Decision making by parents and healthcare professionals when considering continued care for pediatric patients with cancer (Hinds PS, Oakes L, Furman W [1997] *Oncol Nurs Forum* **24**(9): 1523–80). *Oncology Nurses Today* **4**(1): 21

Stevens MM (1995) Family adjustment and support. In: Doyle D, Hanks G, MacDonald N (Eds). *The Oxford Textbook of Palliative Medicine*. Oxford University Press, Oxford: 707–17

Stevens M, Ballantine N, Bradwell M *et al* (2004) Symptom control and palliative care in children with cancer. Unpublished. Departments of Haematology, Oncology and Pharmacy, The Birmingham Children's Hospital NHS Trust. Revised May 2004

Thomas J (1994) Parents. In: Hill L (Ed). *Caring for Dying Children and Their Families*. Chapman and Hall, London: 43–66

Vickers JL, Carlisle C (2000) Choices and control: parental experiences in pediatric terminal home care. *J Pediatr Oncol Nurs* **17**(1): 12–21

Wolfe J (2000) Symptoms and suffering at the end of life in children with cancer. *N Engl J Med* **342**: 326–33

2

Models and organisation of care

Cancer is the the most common disease causing death in children between the ages of one and fourteen years (Chambers and Oakhill, 1995). Paediatric palliative care, however, may be needed for a wide range of conditions (see *Introduction*). The guiding principle behind palliative care for children is to have a variety of services available to meet the individual and differing needs of each family. Children and their families need to be supported in their decision about where the most appropriate location might be to receive care as the child approaches the end of his/her life.

This chapter provides an overview of the various options available to address the different needs of dying children and their families. It focuses on the paediatric oncology model and the role of the West Midlands Paediatric Macmillan Team (WMPMT) in the organisation of care for children dying from a malignant disease.

Models of care

The differences between children and adults make the extension of adult palliative care to children both inappropriate and ineffective. Care providers skilled in the care of dying adults generally lack the expertise to deal with the unique medical and psychosocial needs of children (Morgan and Murphy, 2000). The duration of children's illnesses may be different from that of adults. Palliative care in children may extend from a few months to many years (National Council for Hospice and Specialist Palliative Care Services, Association for Children with Life-Threatening or Terminal Conditions and their Families [ACT] and Association of Children's Hospices [ACH], 2001). The continuing physical, emotional and cognitive development in children sets them apart from adults. It influences all aspects of their care, including pharmacological treatment, their understanding of their disease, communication skills, and their level of dependence.

The organisation and structure of palliative care services for children differ from those of adult services (Morgan and Murphy, 2000). Adult palliative care is often hospice based and consultant led. Paediatric palliative care is provided by a network of agencies across the NHS, the voluntary sector, and social and educational services. Coordination and collaboration between these agencies is essential for the seamless provision of care (Farrell and Sutherland, 1998). Effective collaboration creates a more integrated and holistic service for children and their families, with a wide range of options, more control and an enhanced level of care. A number of locally based models have been developed to care for children with non-malignant life-limiting conditions (NHS Executive, 1998). These palliative care services, led by community paediatricians and multidisciplinary teams, provide mainly respite, home nursing, psychology and social work support (National Council for Hospice and Specialist Palliative Care Services, ACT and ACH, 2001).

One of the significant barriers to providing effective palliative care is the perception that discontinuing aggressive treatment means 'giving up' and 'failure'. The shift in the goal from achieving a cure to making the child comfortable usually occurs only when all other options have been exhausted, reinforcing the myth that palliative care is second best (Morgan and Murphy, 2000). When active cancer treatment has been discontinued, it is important to emphasise to the family that the same high quality care will continue wherever the place of death. If palliative care is to be a success, it is essential that everyone involved in the management – parents, medical staff, nurses and, where appropriate, the child – accepts that the philosophy of treatment should change. One of the important elements of the palliative approach is to offer care in a setting of the child and family's choice.

Paediatric oncology community model

The longest established model is the paediatric oncology model set up for palliative care for children with cancer (National Council for Hospice and Specialist Palliative Care Services, ACT and ACH, 2001). There are, however, some differences in ways of delivering models of paediatric oncology community provision. The different models of practice, structure and organisation depend on the employment location and funding bodies (Hunt, 1995). The main role of the paediatric oncology community nurse, however, is to provide a link between the hospital where the child is receiving care and the child's home, in order to promote a system of seamless care. The way in which this care is delivered will depend on local needs and resources.

Treatment for children with cancer is organised on a regional basis. A highly specialised multidisciplinary team provides the overall care of the child and family, with further care being given by local district hospitals and primary health care teams. Primary care teams without the support of paediatric community nurses may lack the specialist knowledge, medication and equipment needed to offer effective palliative care support to children. Palliative care for children with cancer is based on paediatric oncology nurse specialists working from regional centres or district hospitals, which share care with the cancer centre. Social workers funded by charitable organisations, such as CLIC Sargent Cancer Care for Children, provide psychosocial and financial support to families. Medical support is provided by the paediatric oncologist and haematologists, in collaboration with paediatricians, GPs and occasionally adult palliative care consultants.

The familiar environment of home is usually the preferred place for children dying from cancer and their families (Kohler and Radford 1985; Goldman *et al*, 1990). For the child, this means having as much normal activityand play as possible, together with family members, friends and household pets. For the parents it means they are the primary caregivers. Home enhances their control of the situation and lessens their feeling of helplessness (Sirkia *et al*, 1997). There is also evidence that the long-term problems of bereaved parents and siblings are reduced when the child dies at home, compared with parents who are unable to provide home care (Lauer *et al*, 1989).

The team has found, through experience, that variation in patient age, diagnosis or family structure does not prevent the parents successfully participating in the home care of their dying child. Furthermore, the literature has stated that there are no established criteria that accurately predict a particular family's ability to manage the care of their child at home (Martinson *et al*, 1978; Lauer and Camitta, 1980).

From a global perspective, whether palliative care at home is recommended for children with cancer in general can depend very much on the social support system and structure of their society. In the USA, for example, issues of cost and insurance have to be addressed. Children receiving trial drugs or research protocols may still benefit from a palliative care model at home, but some insurance companies may refuse to pay for both kinds of care. Again, in the USA it may be difficult to receive twenty-four-hour nursing support or intravenous infusion therapy at home because of issues of cost and insurance (Whittam, 1993). Treatments or surgical interventions that improve quality of life or palliate the child's symptoms are usually not reimbursed through the American Medicaid Insurance Benefit Scheme (American Academy of Pediatrics, 2000). European countries such as Finland, despite having private health care, do not charge families for home visits during the palliative phase, and all equipment is provided free of charge (Sirkiä *et al*, 1997).

With support, parents can provide better and more individualised care than many professionals (Whittam, 1993). The ability to fulfil the child's wish to be at home provides the family with a sense of pride and accomplishment (Foley and Whittam, 1990). Families should, however, always have the option of returning to the hospital, without feelings of guilt, if they feel this is necessary or becomes preferable.

Outside of the regional oncology centres, there may be limited opportunity for some medical and nursing staff to gain extensive experience in caring for children dying from a malignancy. This is mainly due to the rarity and sporadic occurrence of childhood malignancies in general. Traditionally, the oncology team has managed the care of the child and family during the palliative phase, providing continuity and the maintenance of ongoing relationships – qualities that may be lost if a completely new team is introduced at this difficult time. GPs may see only one or two children with malignancies in the course of their career, and often feel that they have little experience or training in caring for dying adults, let alone children (Chambers and Oakhill, 1995). For palliative care to be effective, there needs to be flexibility in working practices and collaboration between the regional centres and the community.

Role of the West Midlands Paediatric Macmillan Team

The number of professionals involved during palliative care varies, depending on the needs of the child and family. The role of the WMPMT is to act mainly in an advisory and coordinating capacity. A key aspect of the role is the ability to liaise with the wide variety of professionals involved in the child's care. The team has a major role in facilitating communication and ensuring widespread liaison. Acknowledging each professional's role enables a better partnership in care. A flexible and responsive approach, determined by the needs of the child and family, is adopted. As coordinators of care, the team ensures that lines of communication are kept open and disciplines work together to provide optimum care. This necessitates regular telephone contact and face-to-face meetings with all the disciplines involved in the care of the child and family, particularly during the palliative phase. When the emphasis changes from curative to palliative care, a multidisciplinary team meeting is held. A key member of the primary health care team, who will be instrumental in the care giving, is identified. Information is exchanged and the educational and support needs of the primary healthcare team are identified.

The WMPMT provides a twenty-four-hour on-call telephone advice service (out-of-hours service is provided from 5pm to 8am during the week and continuously throughout the weekend). Each team member in turn is on call. Continuity is ensured by the member being on call for a seven-day period. While on call, the Macmillan nurse provides advice and support to children, families and professionals involved in the care of all palliative patients, the majority of whom may not be directly on her caseload. A weekly multidisciplinary team meeting provides a forum for each Macmillan nurse to present a comprehensive account of symptoms, medication and psychosocial details of every individual child and family on her palliative caseload. This exchange of information is not only essential to inform the on-call Macmillan nurse, but also provides an opportunity for debate, support and teaching.

Cancer and leukaemia in childhood (CLIC) model

There are forty-three paediatric oncology community nursing posts across England, Wales and Scotland funded by the Cancer and Leukaemia in Childhood (CLIC) Trust. One-third of the CLIC nurses work from designated regional paediatric oncology centres, and the remaining two-thirds work from district general hospitals or community bases (CLIC, 2002). The most distinct organisational feature of the CLIC nursing service is their geographical location, with almost three-quarters of CLIC nurses each covering an area of less than thirty-five miles (Hunt, 1996). The CLIC model provides a local service to families, ensuring continuity of care to a small number of patients. A more 'hands-on' approach to care is therefore given by CLIC nurses, who geographically are close at hand for the children and families, both within the hospital setting and in the community (Hunt, 1995).

Community model

Palliative care is increasingly being provided by generic paediatric community nursing services, which have grown in strength and numbers in recent years. Teams, however, vary in size, have heavy caseloads, and many find it difficult to provide the twenty-four-hour palliative care service that families may need. In 1997, only 50% of children in the UK had access to a children's community nursing service, and only 20% of these had access to a twenty-four-hour service (Davies, 1999). By 2000, 70% of children in the UK had access to a paediatric community nurse, still leaving 30% without this provision (National Council for Hospice and Specialist Palliative Care Services, ACT and ACH, 2001).

Diana community teams

In 1999, nine Diana community teams were set up in England and Wales, with a £6 million grant from the NHS to fund the teams over a three-year period. These multidisciplinary nurse-led teams provide home-based family care for all children with life-limiting or life-threatening conditions and their families within a health district. Only nine health districts provide these specialist teams, from a possible 126 (National Council for Hospice and Specialist Palliative Care Services, ACT & ACH, 2001). The Diana teams work with existing services such as children's hospitals, specialist outreach services, children's hospices, social services, education and voluntary agencies. A key element of the service is partnership and cooperation. Their aim is to work across professional and organisational boundaries to provide seamless care (Davies, 1999).

In 2002, the new opportunities fund (NOF), the national lottery good causes distributor, announced details of a £48 million investment for children's palliative care (http://news.bbc.co.uk/1/hi/health/1879897.stm accessed June, 2004). Consequently, in the last two years, the team has seen an increase in community-based children's palliative care services within the West Midlands. As yet, however, not all are providing a twenty-four-hour nursing service.

KEY POINTS

◆ Care of the dying child and family should be provided in the place of their choice.

◆ Care should be provided by professionals that are known to them.

◆ Coordinated, local community nursing and medical support should be available.

◆ Expert specialist advice should be available twenty-four-hours.

◆ There should be a open-door policy regarding hospital facilities.

◆ There should be effective communication between all the agencies involved.

Case study 2.1 (overleaf) illustrates collaboration between adult and paediatric nursing services, in an area where there was only one paediatric community nurse. She worked within a 'paediatric hospital at-home team', whose remit was to provide acute care only to children discharged from the local district general hospital. Issues of funding were paramount in this situation. Her involvement was permitted, as funding of the post came from the community services.

With support and guidance, the adult district nursing team provided a valuable contribution to Jenny's palliative care. In the experience of the team, accessing twenty-four-hour district nursing support can prove difficult. In the absence of a twenty-four-hour paediatric community team, local adult district nursing teams, when approached, might be unwilling to perform clinical procedures for children, feeling it an inappropriate extension of their role (Kirk, 2001).

Case study 2.1

Jenny was diagnosed with metastatic rhabdomyosarcoma at five years of age. The family lived twelve miles from the paediatric oncology centre. One paediatric community nurse (Sarah) was able to be involved in Jenny's care. She met the family at diagnosis and visited regularly to establish a relationship.

When active treatment ceased, a primary health care team meeting was held, which included the paediatric community nurse, members of the adult district nursing team, the GP and the paediatric Macmillan nurse. The use of symptom control medication, equipment, and terminal care guidelines (see *Chapter 5*) was discussed. The meeting was also used as an opportunity to explore the educational needs of the nursing team, in order for them to care for Jenny in the palliative phase.

Following the meeting, joint visits to Jenny took place on a regular basis with Sarah and members of the adult district nursing team to establish relationships. The paediatric Macmillan nurse visited once a week with one member of the district nursing team. Sarah was the daily contact for the family and adult district nurses, with advice and education when necessary from the paediatric Macmillan nurse. As Jenny's symptoms progressed, the evening and night district nursing teams were updated regularly to ensure that the family had access to twenty-four-hour nursing support. The paediatric Macmillan team provided twenty-four-hour telephone support and advice to the family and professionals. Visits were often needed three times a day, including during the evening and overnight. The paediatric Macmillan nurse liaised with the GP to provide appropriate prescriptions for symptom control drugs. The GP visited weekly. Following telephone advice and support from the paediatric Macmillan nurse on call, a subcutaneous syringe driver was set up by the adult district nursing team during the weekend (equipment and prescription ready and available in the house). Jenny died peacefully thirty-six hours later, following a three-month palliative phase.

Potential barriers to the effective provision of palliative care at home

⌘ Professionals receive inadequate training in the management of pain and symptoms.
⌘ Little education on the provision of spiritual support to children and their parents or how to talk about death.
⌘ Lack of scientific understanding of the most effective use of medication and other treatments for palliation.
⌘ Lack of twenty-four-hour community nursing support and specialist advice.

Hospice/respite care model

Improvements in medical care have meant that the lifespan for children and young people with life-limiting conditions has been extended (Davies, 1998). Parents, particularly those caring for children with a degenerative condition, take the major responsibility for providing care for children with complex and demanding medical conditions, with little or no help, sometimes over many years. Respite care is therefore an important feature of the supportive care needed for these families. Respite care is usually thought of as the handing over of care to an individual or service, to allow the carers a break from their responsibilities and/or to allow the person being cared for a break from their carers (Sutherland *et al*, 1993-94).

There has been a steady growth in the number of children's hospices over the last twenty years, the first being Helen House, which opened in Oxford in 1982. There are now twenty-two children's hospices in the UK and a further 16 in the planning stage (National Council for Hospice and Specialist Palliative Care Services, ACT and ACH, 2001). Children's hospices provide flexible, family-centred care throughout the course of the child's illness and after his/her death. They provide respite, emergency, palliative and bereavement support, together with information, advice and practical assistance. This service is provided by multidisciplinary staff, and is available 365 days a year at no cost to the family (ACH, 1995).

The distribution of children's hospices, however, is not related to need, and some families have to travel considerable distances to access a children's hospice (National Council for Hospice and Specialist Palliative Care Services, ACT and ACH, 2001). Children's hospices are charitable organisations and the quality of care provided for children with life-limiting conditions and their families is unlikely to be totally matched by publicly funded organisations such as Social Services or the NHS (Davies, 1998). From a global perspective, the first children's hospice in North America was modelled on Helen House, with others following in the USA, Australia and more recently Germany and Switzerland (Davies, 1998).

Hospice care is an approach to care and not necessarily a physical place. Life and living are the emphasis and can be incorporated into a variety of settings, including the child's home or an inpatient hospital acute care setting. This type of care exists to provide the child and family with support and care so that the child might live fully and comfortably until death (Whittam, 1993). The philosophy is founded on the belief that children and their families should be offered help to achieve a quality of life — physical, emotional and spiritual — throughout a child's lifetime, and to help with bereavement support after the child's death. It is a philosophy that can be translated into community-based care without necessarily having the back-up of a hospice building.

Hospices are used in comparatively few instances for children dying from a malignancy, as most families are not keen to develop new relationships at a late stage of their child's illness, especially if it takes them away from their local community (Goldman *et al*, 1990). Research conducted in the 1980s, soon after the opening of the first children's hospice, found that only 7% of children admitted had cancer-related illnesses. Overton (2001) suggests that this situation continues today. In the experience of the team over a three-year period from May 1999 to 2002, only 4% of children's deaths from a malignancy occurred in local children's hospices (*Figure 2.1*).

Most families prefer their child to be cared for at home, with professional support from those known to them (Chambers and Oakhill, 1995). For some, however, hospital remains their choice of care setting. Families should be allowed to make informed, supported decisions when choosing between home care, hospice and hospital.

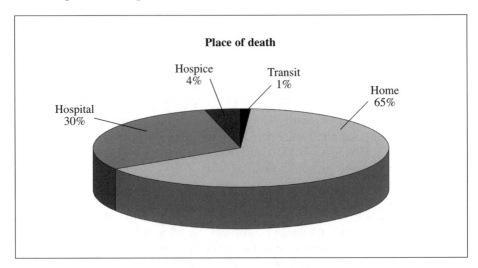

Place of death

Hospice 4%

Transit 1%

Home 65%

Hospital 30%

Figure 2.1: Place of death for children dying from a malignancy in the West Midlands between 1999 and 2002 (Parkes, 2002). NB: Children who died during active treatment are not included in these statistics

Hospital-based model for children dying of a malignancy

Children cared for in the hospital setting are often undergoing curative treatment that renders them acutely ill. The disease may show no response to treatment, leading to progression and subsequent palliation. They may spend little or no time at home during the treatment phase, due to intensive medical intervention that would be difficult to maintain at home. A decision to remain in hospital may therefore seem a natural option. For some, the decision for their child to be in hospital may involve a planned admission or a sudden decision as symptoms change. The reasons for families choosing a hospital setting for the palliative care phase vary. It must be made clear to them that if, at any time, their focus turns to home care, all efforts to accommodate this will be made.

For some families, hospital-based care may be their only option. Practical problems, eg. the parents themselves are unwell or there is little or no family support, can leave the family with limited choices. The complications of the disease process, in particular uncontrolled symptoms or the practicalities of nursing a large adolescent, may mean that hospital care is necessary. Most practical problems preventing home care can be overcome with careful planning, but the wishes of the child and family should be listened to. Families should not be put into a position where they feel compelled to take their child home. Hospice care remains a viable option for some. Many families, however, may not want the introduction of unfamiliar carers at such a difficult time.

Case study 2.2

Zoe, aged fifteen, was receiving palliative care for a brain tumour that had been diagnosed at the age of four years. She required a great deal of physical nursing care from family and professionals, as she was unable to care for herself. The family's home was seventy miles from the regional oncology centre. There was a lack of paediatric community nurses in the area where Zoe and her family lived and no access to a twenty-four-hour community nursing service. Her parents visited a hospice a short distance from their home, but decided that they wanted Zoe to be cared for by the people who knew her well, and with whom she felt comfortable. Zoe died two weeks later on the oncology ward, following a period of rapidly changing physical and psychological symptoms. All her family were present, in an environment that was comfortable and familiar to them all.

For some families, as in *Case study 2.2*, the hospital provides a sense of security and continuity of care from the team with whom they are familiar (Goldman *et al*, 1990). Conversely, other families see it as an environment that is often busy and chaotic. It can create insecurity, discomfort and intrusion, and is an environment that often demands compliance and conformity. It can also leave family members feeling isolated and helpless (Dunne and Sullivan, 2000). Hospitals, particularly those with palliative care teams, have begun to correct such problems.

Emphasis on technology and monitoring is usually unnecessary, and nurses undertaking such tasks need to consider their relevance. If the child has been receiving intensive treatment, eg. bone marrow transplantation, it is likely that a range of interventions have been, and may still be being undertaken. It is not uncommon for the child to be receiving:

- total parenteral nutrition
- intravenous antibiotics
- intravenous fluid
- oxygen
- blood pressure monitoring
- pulse oximetry
- urinary catheterisation, nasogastric feeding or drainage.

It can feel uncomfortable to discuss the removal of medical equipment and drugs with families at such a difficult time. Although nursing and medical staff may worry that it could appear uncaring to do so, steps should be taken to evaluate which of these interventions are essential. Open discussion with the family will help to ensure that such changes are not misinterpreted.

The family should, wherever possible, be able to 'get close' to their child physically and have obstructions preventing them from doing so removed. For example, an oxygen mask that partially obscures the child's face and makes communication difficult may not be necessary at all times. Personalising the environment by removing unnecessary equipment is a simple measure that can be effective in comforting a family. This also demonstrates good basic nursing care in what can easily be seen as an environment where technology and monitoring are prevalent.

For some families, however, the absence of familiar nursing roles, such as temperature taking, may be seen as frightening and neglectful. Careful explanations and negotiation are crucial at this time. Families often feel a loss of control and frustration at the inability to perform family roles when their child is hospitalised prior to death. They should be given as much responsibility as they have been used to, with careful negotiation over drug administration, especially if the families have previously managed care at home.

Together with the physical care of the sick child, the nurse must manage the family's psychosocial needs sensitively when a child is dying. In order for the nurse to fulfil this role, extensive training and support needs to be available in acute areas delivering palliative care. Little attention has been given to the impact that a child's death in hospital has on children's nurses (Costello and Trinder-Brook, 2000). Specific support may not be offered other than that available from peers. As part of their role, the team offers education and support to staff on the oncology unit on issues related to palliative care. Nursing staff who feel confident and supported in their practice will, in turn, convey this confidence to the families in their care.

Although a child's death on a ward can have a significant impact on other families in that setting, the bereaved family should not be rushed into leaving the hospital. They should be encouraged to spend time with their child after his/her death, and be given explanations regarding after-death care, such as where they want their child's body to rest until the funeral (see *Chapter 6*). Families of children cared for at Birmingham Children's Hopital have access to 'The Rainbow Suite' following their child's death. Here, the family can spend as long as they want with their child, in a bedroom-like setting. Hospital staff need to be available to accompany the family to the bedroom. Arrangements can be made with the funeral directors to keep the child's body at the hospital until the funeral, if this is the family's wish.

Parental adjustment following a child's death at home or in hospital has shown marked differences. Lauer *et al* (1989) found that 50% of parents who cared for their child away from the home setting perceived their level of coping to have worsened after their child's death. In contrast, 95% of parents who cared for their child at home asserted that they were coping at the same level or better than before their child's illness. Parents who coped with their child's death at home concluded, in their evaluation, that they had coped 'adequately' or 'very well' at home, whereas the majority of non home-care parents rated their coping as 'inadequate'. More recently, Vickers and Carlisle (2000) suggest that further studies are needed to explore parents' choice and control in the care of their dying child and the ways in which this is linked to their coping strategies. As more parents take their child home to die, further research on parental adaption to the child's death should be conducted. Lauer *et al* (1989) reported a remarkably low incidence of bereavement guilt in the parents who cared for their child at home. Theorists generally believe that guilt can originate from a previous failure to assume responsibility (Buber, 1971). Caring for the dying child at home reduces feelings of parental helplessness by allowing parents to retain control of their environment and thereby assume responsibility (Lauer *et al*, 1989). If the hospital setting is the parental choice for palliative care delivery, every effort should be made to make this as comfortable as possible for the family while empowering them to retain a sense of responsibility and control of the situation.

Families should be offered the opportunity to return later to the hospital to meet their child's consultant, regardless of where they were cared for in the palliative phase. This gives them the opportunity to ask any questions or express any concerns that they may have. Consideration needs to be given regarding the venue for this meeting, as some families will not want to return to the ward or clinic environment.

Summary

From the models described in this chapter, it is possible to establish the elements necessary for an effective service that will meet the needs of most children dying of a malignancy and their families. There will always be some children and conditions that require hospital care and these should not be seen as failures. In the experience of the WMPMT, hospital deaths in the palliative care phase have largely been due to the sudden and unpredictable escalation of symptoms. Children's hospices undoubtedly provide quality care for children with life-limiting conditions and their families, but being charitable organisations, they have not yet been planned on a national scale, leaving some communities without this specialised care.

The importance of resources in the community cannot be underestimated. Ongoing communication between the oncology providers, community providers and the family keeps everyone informed and promotes collaborative working. The need for seamless care requires effective collaboration of all the care agencies. As illustrated in this chapter, the process of collaboration consists of the development of partnerships in care for the wellbeing of the child dying from a malignancy and his/her family. Through collaboration, families of children dying of cancer are given choices. Families can then at least accept or reject services on the basis of informed consent.

It is essential that the family has access to twenty-four-hour medical and nursing support. How this is planned will depend on local arrangements and professional support. Formal training in palliative care for children with a malignancy, although increasing, is not yet widely available and this has a bearing on the standard of care available within each model discussed in this chapter.

Management of the terminal phase of the child's illness has a dramatic effect on the psychosocial recovery of the family (Whittam, 1993). Never will a child and family be more in need of compassionate and expert care than when they reach the palliative phase of the disease. It is the responsibility of professionals to ensure that this time in the family and child's life is managed appropriately wherever they choose to receive care.

References

American Academy of Pediatrics (2000) Policy Statement: Palliative Care for Children (RE0007) *Pediatrics* **106** (2): 351–7

Association of Children's Hospices (1995) *Guidelines for Good Practice in a Children's Hospice.* ACH, London

Buber M (1971) Existential guilt. In: Smith R (Ed). *Guilt: Man and Society.* Doubleday and co, New York. Cited in: Lauer M, Muchern R *et al* (1989) Long-term follow-up of paternal adjustment following a child's death at home or hospital. *Cancer* **4**(63): 988–94

Cancer and Leukaemia in Childhood (CLIC) (2002) available from http://www.clic.uk.com (accessed 27 June 2002)

Chambers EJ, Oakhill A (1995) Models of care for children dying of malignant disease. *Palliat Med* **9**: 181–5

Costello J, Trinder-Brook A (2000) Children's nurses' experiences of caring for dying children in hospital. *Paediatr Nurs* **12**(6): 28–32

Davies RE (1998) The growth of hospices in the UK. *Paediatr Nurs* **10**(8): 23–6

Davies RE (1999) The Diana community nursing team and paediatric palliative care. *Br J Nurs* **8**(8): 506, 508–511

Dunne K, Sullivan K (2000) Family experiences of palliative care in the acute hospital setting. *Int J Palliat Nurs* **6**(4): 170–8

Farrell M, Sutherland P (1998) Providing paediatric palliative care: collaboration in practice. *Br J Nurs* **7**(12): 712–16

Foley GV, Whittam EH (1990) Care of the child dying of cancer: I. *CA Cancer J Clin* **40**: 327–54

Goldman A, Beardsmore S, Hunt J (1990) Palliative care for children with cancer – home, hospital or hospice? *Arch Dis Child* **65**: 641–3

Hunt J (1995) The paediatric community nurse specialist: the influence of employment location and funders of practice. *J Adv Nurs* **22**(1): 126–33

Hunt J (1996) *Paediatric Oncology Outreach Nurse Specialists: The Impact of Funding Arrangements on their Professional Relationships.* A report to The Paediatric Oncology Nurses Forum, Royal College of Nursing, London, and the United Kingdom Children's Cancer Study Group, Leicester

Kirk S (2001) Negotiating lay and professional roles in the care of children with complex health care needs. *J Adv Nurs* **34**(5): 593–602

Kohler JA, Radford M (1985) Terminal care for children dying of cancer: quantity and quality of life. *Br Med J (Clin Res Ed)* **291**: 115–16

Lauer ME, Camitta BM (1980) Home care for dying children: a nursing model. *J Pediatr* **97**(6): 1032–5

Lauer ME, Mulhern RK, Schell MJ, Camitta BM (1989) Long-term follow-up of parental adjustment following a child's death at home or hospital. *Cancer* **63**(5): 988–94

Martinson IM, Armstrong GD, Geis DP *et al* (1978) Facilitating home care for children dying of cancer. *Cancer Nurs* **1**(1): 41–5

Morgan E, Murphy S (2000) Care of children who are dying of cancer. *N Engl J Med* **342**(5): 347–8

National Council for Hospice and Specialist Palliative Care Services, Association for Children with Life-Threatening or Terminal Conditions and their Families (ACT) and Association of Children's Hospices (ACH) (2001) *Joint Briefing: Palliative Care for Children.* Number 1, April 2001

NHS Executive (1998) *Evaluation of the Pilot Project Programme for Children with Life-Threatening Illnesses.* HMSO, London

Overton J (2001) The development of children's hospices in the UK. *Eur J Palliat Care* **8**(1): 30–3

Parkes S (2002) *Tumour Registry.* Birmingham Children's Hospital, Birmingham

Sirkiä K, Saarinen UM, Ahlgren B, Hovi L (1997) Terminal care of the child with cancer at home. *Acta Paediatr* **86**(10): 1125–3

Sutherland R, Hearn J, Baum D, Elston S (1993–94) Definitions in paediatric palliative care. *Health Trends* **25**(4): 148–50

Vickers J, Carlisle, C (2000) Choices and control: parental experiences in pediatric terminal home care. *J Pediatr Oncol Nurs* **17**(1): 12–21

Whittam EH (1993) Terminal care of the dying child. Psychosocial implications of care. *Cancer* **71**(10 Suppl): 3450–62

3

Active treatment in paediatric palliative care

The aim of palliation is to optimise quality of life in the absence of curative treatment for progressive disease. One method of achieving this is to utilise treatment modalities that are primarily used as curative treatments. Modification of radiotherapy, chemotherapy and surgery means that these treatments can be used effectively to achieve symptomatic relief in the palliative phase of care. This chapter will consider such modalities, including phase I and II clinical trial studies.

During the palliative phase of treatment, healthcare professionals should encourage open discussion of the potential benefits and adverse effects of any therapy being considered, thereby enabling families to make informed choices. Families should be made aware that they are not compelled to abide by any decision made, and can withdraw from treatment at any time if they feel it is not beneficial to their child.

A consistent approach to discussions helps to prevent families receiving mixed messages about the expectations of the therapies employed. To minimise the risk of families developing unrealistic expectations, healthcare professionals should ensure that the child and family remain aware of the palliative nature of such interventions. Families who choose active treatments in palliation may believe that the longer their child survives, the more likely it is that a 'miracle', new or curative treatment will present. They may also assume that a significant improvement in their child's condition indicates a further remission and changes the long-term prognosis, leading them to question previous medical opinions. It is important to help them understand that, although the response is what was hoped for, treatment remains palliative not curative.

Palliative radiotherapy

Radiotherapy can alleviate some of the distressing symptoms caused by progressive disease. The benefits of radiotherapy to the child, however, must outweigh the negative impact that this has in terms of lost time, distress, discomfort and the financial and emotional costs incurred by extra journeys to the treatment centre. Healthcare professionals must ensure, as far as is practicable, that the child and parents participate actively in the decision-making process to undertake such treatment.

Curative radiotherapy is usually delivered in daily fractions, with the total treatment course taking between two and six weeks. The impact of such lengthy treatment is usually hard to justify for the child with a limited life expectancy. It has been established that a single dose or a short course of radiotherapy is as effective as intensive fractionated treatment in achieving symptom relief in palliative care (Crellin *et al*, 1989; Medical Research Council, 1991; Goldman, 1992; Hoskin, 1995).

Nevertheless, this modality of treatment may necessitate further hospital visits for consent, treatment planning and simulation as well as the delivery of radiotherapy. As it is still considered most appropriate for palliative radiotherapy to be given at a regional centre, families may have to travel significant distances (see *Introduction*). Paediatric palliative radiotherapy is therefore planned so as to minimise the number of hospital visits required. In some cases it has been possible to achieve planning, simulation and delivery of radiotherapy in one session.

Radiotherapy can be a frightening experience for children and adults alike. For the uncooperative child, radiotherapy can be distressing. The preparation of the child for the procedure must remain a high priority. Play therapists are invaluable in familiarising the child and family with the treatment, equipment used and the procedure itself. The use of a general anaesthetic will be necessary for the young child undergoing radiotherapy.

The following section considers symptoms of paediatric malignancy that are particularly amenable to radiotherapy.

Pain

Bone metastases are one of the most common causes of cancer pain (Finegan, 1999). Bone pain is commonly treated with non-steroidal anti-inflammatory drugs (NSAIDs) and opiates. As bone pain is only partially responsive to opiates and NSAIDs have a recognised ceiling dose, radiotherapy may be the treatment of choice for pain arising from bone metastases (Brady, 1994; Hoskin, 1995; Janjan, 2001). The reasons why bone metastases cause such intense pain, and the mechanisms by which radiotherapy achieves pain control (Hopkins and Pownall, 1999), are not completely understood. However, adult studies report a response rate of 80–90%, with complete control of pain in 50–60% (Hoskin, 1995; Finegan, 1999). The full effect of treatment may not be observed for up to two to three weeks, therefore regular pain assessment and adequate analgesia during this period are essential, until analgesia can be reduced as pain resolves. Because of this delay in analgesic effect, radiotherapy may not be the treatment of choice in children with a very short prognosis. In paediatric palliative care, painful bone metastases are often associated with solid tumours such as osteosarcoma and neuroblastoma, but also appear to respond well to radiotherapy.

For children with multiple painful lesions, more than one course of radiotherapy can be considered. However, repeated use of palliative radiotherapy at different sites in the body will be costly in terms of the child and family's physical and emotional resources. Good multiprofessional assessment should determine in advance whether any course under consideration is justified.

Pathological fracture

Pathological fractures can occur spontaneously in diseased bone as a result of minor trauma. Sudden onset of pain upon movement may indicate the presence of pathological fracture, and on examination there may be swelling, local pain and deformity (Regnard and Tempest, 1992). Radiotherapy can help both the prevention and treatment of such fractures (Hoskin, 1995), with fractionated radiotherapy being considered more effective than a single fraction (Hopkins and Pownall, 1999). This occurs through the promotion of recalcification of bone at the site of metastases, thereby improving the structural integrity of the bone in the medium term. Another treatment option for pathological fracture is surgical internal fixation. This may not always be a feasible option, eg. in the case of vertebral collapse or fracture of the pelvis, and hence radiotherapy may be used alone.

Compression

Neurological deficit due to compression of the spinal cord can result from metastases within or outside the spinal cord (intradural or extradural), or collapse or instability of the spine as a result of vertebral metastasis. Spinal cord compression should be identified and treated quickly. If spinal cord compression is suspected, corticosteroids should be commenced as emergency treatment before the initiation of radiotherapy, and continued until its completion (Hoskin, 1995).

A prompt referral to, and treatment by, a radiotherapist is essential if longer-term problems are to be prevented (Hoskin, 1995). Even when the prognosis is short, prevention of paralysis remains a high priority in order to maintain the dignity and quality of life of the dying child.

Prophylactic radiotherapy should be considered for patients identified as being at high risk of developing spinal cord involvement (Hoskin, 1995). However, not all children who develop spinal cord compression have identified spinal lesions, making prevention difficult. The inability of the younger child to verbalise unusual sensations such as 'pins and needles' or difficulty in passing urine, can result in delayed diagnosis.

Direct tumour compression and infiltration leading to nerve compression and subsequent nerve pain is symptomatically challenging. Local irradiation to the tumour site may be indicated if the use of secondary analgesics, such as anticonvulsants, corticosteroids and antidepressants, has failed to achieve control.

Case study 3.1 illustrates the use of fractionated radiotherapy for vertebral collapse, cord and nerve compression.

Case study 3.1

Toni, a fifteen-year-old girl, was diagnosed with metastatic primitive neuroectodermal tumour, the primary disease being in her pelvis. Both Toni and her family were aware from the outset that the chance of cure was very poor. Despite intensive chemotherapy, Toni's disease progressed. She experienced neuropathic pain in her left leg as a result of nerve compression from her primary disease. Despite adjuvant analgesia in the form of anticonvulsants and a short course of corticosteroids, the pain remained unresolved. The decision was made with the family to treat the primary site of disease with palliative radiotherapy. Immediately before this treatment was administered, Toni developed back pain, which became more intense on movement, and altered sensation in her legs. X-ray confirmed pathological fracture of L1 and L2. Radiotherapy was administered over 5 days to her spine and pelvis. Toni died seven days after completion of radiotherapy. Her pain never fully resolved. Although she wanted to have the treatment, Toni resented the time she spent at hospital, when her priority was to spend time with her mother and friends.

This case illustrates the dilemma of deciding whether the physical and emotional upheaval associated with radiotherapy is justified. Had Toni lived longer, the benefits of the radiotherapy in terms of her physical independence may well have enhanced her quality of life.

Distant metastases

Radiotherapy plays an important role in relieving symptoms arising from metastatic disease. Cerebral metastases, for example, may present with headache, confusion, neurological impairment, nausea and seizures. Corticosteroids provide short-term relief but are often associated with significant side-effects. Radiotherapy is a well-established, effective palliative treatment for cerebral metastases in adults. A short course of radiotherapy is usually sufficient to reduce the metastasis and any associated cerebral oedema. Hoskin (1995) reports an 80% response rate in treating headache, confusion and motor and sensory loss.

Palliative chemotherapy

The aim of chemotherapy in palliative care is to provide good symptom control for the child, while minimising the negative impact of toxicities and the demands of administration.

Toxicity

The short-term side-effects of chemotherapeutic agents that are justifiable during curative treatment are generally not acceptable in the palliative phase of treatment. Conversely, the risk of late effects or delayed toxicity does not present a major concern (Holmes, 1990).

For those children who endured distressing side-effects during curative chemotherapy, their previous experience may influence their view about undertaking a further course of chemotherapy. For some the word 'chemotherapy' generates such awful memories that they will not even consider better-tolerated palliative agents, such as oral etoposide or mercaptopurine. Chemotherapy regimens that incur significant bone marrow suppression are generally avoided as they increase the risk of febrile neutropenia, necessitating hospitalisation and the need for blood product transfusion — interventions that impact on the child's remaining quality time.

The side-effects of chemotherapy pose an enormous threat to body image, independence and self-control of the child and adolescent (Wilkinson-Carr, 2000). For the older child or adolescent, the visual impact of having little or no hair can restrict their socialisation for fear of being seen as different from their peers — a factor that can rule palliative chemotherapy out of the equation.

Palatability

The use of oral chemotherapy requires compliance from the child. For some children, oral chemotherapy is an acceptable method of administration, whereas for others it can become very problematic.

The preparations of oral chemotherapy available can impact on the decision of children and their families to continue with treatment. The administration of oral etoposide, frequently used in palliation, can create conflict between parent and child. In capsule form it is large, and in its liquid state oily and virtually impossible to disguise. Occasionally the child may already have a nasogastric tube in place, and this can alleviate some of the difficulties associated with drug administration. Some families even request the insertion of a nasogastric tube for this purpose; this may, however, create an ethical dilemma for carers if the child refuses.

Careful discussion and negotiation with both the child and his/her family must take place when such conflict arises, to ensure that the best interests of the child are being considered.

Venous access

Chemotherapeutic agents such as vincristine and vinblastine require venous administration and therefore venous access. The child may still have a central venous access device in place if disease progression has occurred while he/she was receiving curative treatment; however, this is unlikely if curative treatment ceased sometime before relapse.

For the child with a needle phobia, regular venepunctures are an unattractive option. It is not unknown for children to elect to have central venous access devices reinserted. Obviously, this is hard to justify in the child who has a short life expectancy, with insertion requiring hospitalisation and a general anaesthetic, and carrying a risk of infection.

Clinic/hospital attendance

Chemotherapy generally necessitates a time commitment from the family to allow administration and monitoring. In some cases, such as the administration of intrathecal chemotherapy for symptomatic relief in children with leukaemic infiltration of their central nervous system, hospital visits are unavoidable.

However, other regimens can be planned to minimise the number of visits to the treatment centre. For example, the use of oral etoposide requires monitoring of full blood counts and physical examination before each course, necessitating only a monthly hospital appointment. The ability of primary health care teams or local hospitals to check full blood counts can help families avoid unnecessary journeys to the treatment centre.

Discontinuation of chemotherapy

Withdrawal of palliative chemotherapy should be considered whenever there is evidence of disease progression or significant side-effects are experienced. In their study of palliative chemotherapy treatment decisions in adults, Detmar *et al* (2002) found that 70% of patients continued to receive their planned treatment despite seriously impaired health-related quality of life. In the paediatric setting, some families find it equally difficult to reach the decision to stop palliative chemotherapy.

Case study 3.2

Robert, aged five years, suffered a relapse of his neuroblastoma, with evidence of several sites of disease. At the time, Robert was well and lively and his parents found it impossible to accept the short prognosis they were given. The family begged Robert's consultant to seek new treatments for him, but eventually agreed to oral etoposide in the belief that this might hold Robert's disease until new treatment became available. The family brought many articles from newspapers and the internet detailing new anticancer agents for discussion with the medical team. Robert remained well for the first few weeks on oral etoposide, but then showed evidence of low blood counts and needed admission for intravenous antibiotics to treat a severe chest infection. Before discharge, further bony lesions were noted on Robert's scalp and these continued to increase in size despite a further course of oral etoposide. His parents pleaded with professionals to continue the etoposide, as they believed that a lesion on his arm was starting to shrink. A fortnight into the third course of etoposide, following a hospital admission with severe mucositis, the family agreed to discontinue the drug, putting their faith in a herbal remedy until Robert died three weeks later.

As in *Case study 3.2*, parents may believe that, despite signs of disease progression, the disease would be advancing more quickly without the chemotherapy. Others, reliant on the possibility of a potentially new curative treatment becoming available, hope that the chemotherapy will keep their child well in the interim. Families have sometimes vocalised the belief that to stop chemotherapy is to 'give up' on their child. For some of these families, the belief has been so strong that oral chemotherapy is administered by parents right up until the day of death, despite clear evidence of progressive disease.

Palliative surgery

For children with advancing disease, particularly solid tumours, it is important to involve surgical colleagues. Surgery may be used to relieve an existing symptom (eg. surgical removal of tumours causing bowel obstruction), prevent anticipated symptoms (eg. removal of lung metastases) or prolong life (eg. debulking of cerebral tumours). Surgical procedures may afford benefit in all these areas (eg. decompression of the spinal cord compression).

As with any treatment, the views of the child and family are paramount in establishing whether the proposed intervention is the treatment of choice. Children usually have firm views on the treatments they find tolerable, and provided that these decisions are based on accurate understanding of the treatment, its benefits and risks, such views should be respected. Some children who have coped well with surgery have had further surgical interventions when required. For example, sequential thoracotomies to remove multiple lung metastases have provided children with good palliation. *Case study 3.3* is an example of a discrete lesion causing life-threatening symptoms, justifying quite major surgery.

Case study 3.3

Tom, a five-year-old boy, suffered a relapse of his abdominal rhabdomyosarcoma and progression of tumour despite further chemotherapy. The tumour caused a pyloric obstruction. The decision was made to perform a surgical bypass of the tumour and create a gastrojejunostomy to facilitate enteral feeding. This procedure helped Tom return to a good state of nutrition and health for a further four months.

Because of the need for hospitalisation, and a likely worsening of symptoms in the initial postoperative period, particularly careful consideration should be given to surgery proposed in a child expected to have a very short prognosis.

Corticosteroids

Although corticosteroids have widespread application in symptom management in paediatric malignancy, eg. for raised intracranial pressure, bone invasion and nerve compression, their role is controversial (Bouffet, 2000). They can provide good initial symptom control (Brady, 1994); however, the long-term side-effects often result in distress for the child and family. Practice has highlighted how quickly children become cushingoid. Young people are image conscious, therefore rapid weight gain and skin changes leading to altered body image are unacceptable to many of them. Labile mood and behaviour changes may also be distressing for both the child and family (Stevens *et al*, 1999). Commencement of steroids for palliative symptom control should therefore only be contemplated after careful consideration and exhaustive manipulation of other medication.

A more difficult issue is discontinuation of steroids once they have been introduced. If initiated in the palliative phase, a detailed explanation about the potential severity of side-effects should be given, and a plan should be agreed with the family for a defined course, preferably of short, sharp duration. Such pulsed therapy will minimise side-effects and can eliminate the need for gradual dose reduction. Furthermore, it will reduce the risk of doses being increased again as symptoms break through, resulting in continued administration of steroids during palliation. Although much discussed as the best treatment option (Walker *et al*, 1999), pulsed steroid treatment is used infrequently, and even when a pulsed regimen is intended it may not be adhered to. Specific discussion and education about this issue, illustrating the benefits alongside a defined plan for stopping the steroid, may promote greater compliance in both family and professionals.

For some diseases, however, the use of steroids will already be established as part of disease management. Children who have endocrine abnormalities as a result of their disease or treatment may receive replacement hydrocortisone, and children suffering from brain tumours may require dexamethasone to reduce oedema during radiotherapy. For children with brainstem gliomas it is often extremely difficult to withdraw dexamethasone post-treatment. The very slow reduction in dosage that they require may mean that dexamethasone is still in use when the child relapses. Although discontinuation of the steroids is desirable, in such situations it may be impossible.

Clinical trials

The media regularly report new breakthroughs in cancer treatments. For the family who has been told that their child has incurable disease, such reports offer hope of the miracle they have been wishing for. Practitioners involved in palliative care are frequently approached with extracts from newspapers and website reports of new treatments. Families require full and frank discussion about the treatments they have identified. This will often provide an opening for further discussion about treatments available in the UK. This section will describe how new, experimental treatments are tested in clinical trials, and the practical and ethical dilemmas that families face when considering their child's participation in such trials.

In the UK, experimental treatments are controlled by a number of professional bodies, including the United Kingdom Children's Cancer Study Group (UKCCSG), the Medical Research Council (MRC) and the Association of the British Pharmaceutical Industry (ABPI). Clinical trials are the scientifically approved method used by these agencies to evaluate new treatments. Terracini *et al* (2001) report an improvement in cure rates for childhood cancer to 70% in Europe. It can be argued that much of the progress to date has been due to systematic testing in clinical trials (Murphy, 2001).

Studies are designed to ensure that scientific data are collected as swiftly as possible, recruiting the minimum number of children, but ensuring scientifically valid results (Hooker, 1999). Approval for the trial has to be obtained from either a local research ethics committee (LREC) or a multicentre research ethics committee (MREC) before it can take place.

Phase I trials

Phase I studies are the first trials in humans. New agents will have satisfied extensive safety and efficacy testing in preclinical tests, including laboratory and animal studies. Some knowledge of the degree of activity and toxicity will be gained from adult trials. It is only following these investigations that a trial is undertaken in the paediatric population. The main aim of phase I trials is to determine the maximum tolerated dose (MTD) and the dose-limiting toxicities (DLT) (Kodish *et al*, 1992).

The results of adult trials cannot easily or accurately be transferred to children, as their tolerance of an agent often differs from that of an adult (Pratt, 1991). Paediatric phase I trials often have a starting dose at 80% of the MLD established in adults (Leventhal, 1994). Children are eligible for recruitment onto a phase I trial if they have relapsed following all standard therapies or have not responded to treatment. During the trial the dose is escalated in mathematically defined increments. Three children are entered at each dose level and observed for related toxicities. This continues in the absence of any unacceptable toxicity until the MTD and DLT are defined. Regular pharmacokinetic data are usually collected with a series of blood and urine sampling to identify the drug's absorption, bioavailability and excretion (Hooker, 1999). Each child is entered at one dose level only; for some the dose may provide symptom relief or a disease response.

Phase II trials

Once the MTD and DLT have been established in phase I trials, the new agent can be investigated further to determine anti-tumour activity. Phase II trials aim to determine the efficacy of the new agent in a particular tumour type or types. Children entered into phase II trials normally have relapsed or have progressive disease after receiving standard treatment. The MTD of the new agent is administered to a defined number of children. Phase II trials not only allow the response of the disease to the drug to be measured, but also enable further toxicity investigations, pharmacological studies and the testing of a particular scheme of administration. Phase II trials ultimately provide evidence about the suitability of the new agent for further randomised phase III trials to determine its value against standard therapy. Children who experience some benefit and limited toxicity from a new agent in phase I or II studies will usually be allowed to continue therapy.

Ethical considerations

The terminally ill child and their family are often rendered extremely vulnerable by their desperation to find any treatment that offers a chance of cure or prolonged survival. Such desperation can skew the family's judgment and lead them to pursue avenues that are not necessarily in the best interests of their child. Paediatric oncologists and haematologists have expressed concern about parents' reasons for agreeing to phase I trials, fearing that the need to maintain hope, as well as an inability to stop treatment, are among parent's reasons for trial entry (Estlin *et al*, 2000).

The process of providing informed consent for trial entry must address many difficult topics. The family must be aware that the primary aim of the trial is to provide information about the new drug, and that therapeutic benefit may well not be observed. Estlin *et al* (2000) reported an overall response to phase I agents in only 10% of patients in paediatric phase I trials and these were mostly partial responses. It is also important that the family appreciate the costs of the trial in terms of travel and hospital commitments, and the likelihood of side-effects (although only 1% of children experienced toxicity in the Estlin series).

Some studies, as in *Case study 3.4*, request trial entry with realistic expectations that the new drug may allow their child some extra time, but do not expect a cure. Some family members, like Georgina's grandparents, have high hopes that new drugs may eradicate the disease. They can be so driven by the prospect of cure that they appear unable to make an assessment of the relative costs and benefits of trial entry for their child. However, in bereavement these families express the belief that they did everything to try to save their child and that their child fought until the very end. In this case study, the family had no regrets about trial entry; however, had Georgina suffered debilitating side-effects, the family may have felt differently, which may in turn have had an effect on their grieving.

Case study 3.4

Georgina's leukaemia had persisted, despite an originally good prognosis, first-line treatment and bone marrow transplantation at relapse. Her parents quickly accepted that treatment was now palliative. Georgina's grandparents, although supportive, felt that there must be other things that could help Georgina's prognosis and found details, on the internet, of a new agent being trialled for children with leukaemia. Georgina's parents approached their consultant, who confirmed that she would be eligible for inclusion in the trial, but would have to attend another centre to do this.

Following lengthy discussion of the likely costs and benefits of the trial drug, the family travelled to a treatment centre coordinating the trial, where Georgina spent a total of a fortnight completing the required investigations and receiving the drug. Georgina remained well throughout, but had dramatic evidence of disease progression three weeks later and died within a few days. Georgina's family felt that the trial drug had done nothing to delay progression of the disease but did not regret their decision to enter the trial, as Georgina had not been troubled by side-effects. Her parents also felt that they would always have wondered what benefits the drug might have brought, had they not tried it.

The child's active participation in the research consent process should be positively encouraged (Devine, 2001), even if conflicts arise between parent and child. Factors considered by children when deciding whether to participate in experimental treatment have been identified (Nitschke *et al,* 1982), and include the following:

- hope for remission
- separation from home
- painful procedures
- side-effects of the drugs.

Organisation

Most clinical trials require the child to undertake a timetable of frequent monitoring, and there is therefore a risk that trial obligations will take precedence over good palliation of symptoms. Effective links between palliative care and research teams enable trial requirements to be met while any symptoms are managed. However, the need for trials to be coordinated at other centres can introduce practical difficulties in communication between teams.

Complementary therapies

Complementary therapies are treatments or practices that are used in conjunction with conventional medicine. The term 'complementary therapy' covers a wide range of therapies, including aromatherapy, massage, herbal remedies and visualisation. Families utilise complementary therapies during both active treatment and palliative care.

Families who are interested in complementary therapies should discuss this with their doctor at the earliest opportunity. The aim of such consultation should be to ensure the safety of the child without being dismissive of therapies under discussion. Healthcare professionals should endeavour to maintain the partnership with the family, ensuring that families do not consider it necessary to be secretive about other therapies they are giving or have arranged for their child. They should be supported in their decision and guided to professionally accredited practitioners. For families returning from abroad with therapies such as herbal remedies it may be necessary to examine the remedy to ensure that its components are not contraindicated by current medication.

Macmillan Cancer Relief (2002) has published a *Directory of Complementary Therapy Services in UK Cancer Care,* which also highlights plans for the development of national guidelines for the use of complementary therapies in palliative care. This may provide a helpful guide for families.

Summary

A variety of treatment modalities can be employed in palliation, including surgery, radiotherapy and chemotherapy. Such active treatments have the potential to prolong life, but this is a secondary consideration if the quality of life is adversely affected by the proposed treatment. The aim is to relieve symptoms as quickly as possible with minimal intervention and toxicity. The benefits and adverse effects of any regimen undertaken should be regularly re-evaluated to ensure that continuation of treatment remains worthwhile.

It is important to consider the individual views of the child and family in deciding whether active treatment should be undertaken. The transition from curative to palliative care will rarely be straightforward, and communication skills are paramount in helping the family to establish the best treatment plan for their child.

References

Bouffet E (2000) Common brain tumours in children: diagnosis and treatment. *Paediatr Drugs* Jan-Feb **2**(1): 57–66

Brady M (1994) Symptom control in dying children. In: Hill L (Ed). *Caring for Dying Children and Their Families*. Chapman and Hall, London: 123–61

Crellin AM, Marks A, Maher EJ (1989) Why don't British radiologists give single fractions of radiotherapy for bony metastases? *Clin Oncol* **1**(2): 63–6

Detmar SB, Muller MJ, Schornagel JH *et al* (2002) Role of health-related quality of life in palliative chemotherapy treatment decisions. *J Clin Oncol* **20**(4): 1056–62

Devine T (2001) Presenting a case for involving children with a terminal illness in clinical trials. *Int J Palliat Nurs* **7**(10): 482–4

Estlin EJ, Cotterill S, Pratt CB *et al* (2000) Phase I trials in pediatric oncology: perceptions of pediatricians from the United Kingdom Children's Cancer Study Group and the Pediatric Oncology Group. *J Clin Oncol* **18**(9): 1900–5

Finegan WC (Ed) (1999) *Helpful Essential Links to Palliative Care*. 3rd edn. Macmillan Cancer Relief, London

Goldman A (1992) Care of the dying child. In: Plowman PN, Pinkerton CR (Eds). *Paediatric Oncology: Clinical Practice and Controversies*. Chapman and Hall, London: 618–30

Holmes S (1990) *Cancer Chemotherapy*. The Lisa Sainsbury Foundation, London

Hooker L (1999) Future trends. In: Gibson F, Evans M (Eds). *Paediatric Oncology: Acute nursing care*. Whurr Publishers, London

Hopkins M, Pownall J (1999) The role of radiotherapy in palliation. In: Gibson F, Evans M (Eds). *Paediatric Oncology: Acute nursing care*. Whurr Publishers, London

Hoskin PJ (1995) Radiotherapy in symptom management. In: Doyle D, Hanks N, MacDonald N (Eds). *Oxford Textbook Of Palliative Medicine*. Oxford University Press, Oxford: 117–29

Janjan N (2001) Bone metastases: approaches to management. *Semin Oncol* **28**(4, Suppl 11): 28–34

Kodish E, Stocking C, Ratain MJ *et al* (1992) Ethical issues in phase I oncology research: a comparison of investigators and institutional review board chairmans. *J Clin Oncol* **10**(11): 1810–16

Leventhal BG (1994) Clinical trials in pediatric oncology. In: Pochedly C (Ed). *Neoplastic Diseases of Childhood: Volume 1*. Harwood Academic Publishers, GmbH, Chur, Switzerland: 101–10

Macmillan Cancer Relief (2002) *Directory of Complementary Therapy Services in UK Cancer Care*. Macmillan Cancer Relief and Cambridge Publishers, London

Medical Research Council (1991) Randomised trials of palliative radiotherapy with ten or two fractions. *Br J Cancer* **63**(2): 265–70

Murphy SB (2001) Cancer clinical trials: risks and benefits. *J Pediatr Hematol Oncol* **23**(9): 564–7

Nitschke R, Humphrey GB, Sexauer CL *et al* (1982) Therapeutic choices made by patients with end-stage cancer. *J Pediatr* **101**(3): 471–6

Pratt CB (1991) The conduct of phase I-II clinical trials in children with cancer. *Med Pediatr Oncol* **19**(4): 304–9

Regnard CFB, Tempest S (1992) *A Guide to Symptom Relief in Advanced Cancer*. 4th edn. Hochland and Hochland Ltd, Hale, Cheshire

Stevens M, Ballantine N, Bradwell M *et al*. Symptom control and palliative care in children with cancer. Unpublished. Departments of Haematology, Oncology and Pharmacy, The Birmingham Children's Hospital NHS Trust. Revised May 1999

Terracini B, Coeburgh JW, Gatta G *et al* (2001) Childhood cancer survival in Europe: an overview. *Eur J Cancer* **37**(6): 810–6

Walker DA, Punt JAG, Sokal M (1999) Clinical management of brain stem glioma. *Arch Dis Child* **80**(6): 558–64

Wilkinson-Carr K (2000) Psychological impact of treatment. In: Langton H (Ed). *The Child with Cancer: Family-centred care in practice*. Harcourt Publishers, Edinburgh: 79–104

4

Talking about children dying

Within paediatric palliative care, the need for effective and skilled communication techniques is unequivocal. In their study of children with life-threatening illnesses, Woolley *et al* (1989) report that the style of communication in a single interview can remain with a family for many years. Families often recount stories of how they were told about their child's impending death and the effectiveness of professionals in relaying concern and information. It is clear that the impact of professionals' approach can have long-term effects.

The ability to communicate bad news effectively has been likened to an art form (Lloyd-Williams, 2002). It is a challenging area of practice that requires the input of a skilled practitioner. What professionals think they are saying, and what families are hearing, may be different. The words used and the subtlety of language may make the message ambiguous.

Delivering the news that a child is no longer curable is never easy, however many times one is faced with this situation. Likewise, maintaining open communication with the child, family and community during palliation is challenging, and subject to many influences.

This chapter will discuss these influences and suggest strategies for improving communication and supporting individuals. Evidence from the literature and the experience of the West Midlands Paediatric Macmillan Team (WMPMT) will be utilised. The chapter is divided into four main sections:

⌘ Talking with parents and families.
⌘ Talking with children.
⌘ Talking with school.
⌘ Talking among professionals.

Talking with parents and families

Relationships between professionals and family members need firm underpinnings. Sincerity, respect and mutual trust are the cornerstones from which effective relationships can be built. Respect can be demonstrated through a true desire to learn from the unique experiences of each family member.

The ability of professionals to allocate time and consideration to the communication process is crucial. A family will often need more than one consultation with their care team to discuss fully the change from curative to palliative care. Professionals must be prepared to reiterate information and constantly reassess the family's understanding. Finding ways to help parents understand such a prognosis, while ensuring that a good relationship with them is retained, can be like walking a tightrope. Pushing the parent too hard into accepting that death is inevitable may cause the parent to withdraw from any relationship with professionals, to the potential detriment of the whole family (Stevens and O'Riordan, 1996). Yet to collude with an unrealistic goal of cure will, in itself, inhibit good palliative care. Good communication skills are pivotal.

In their North American study, Wolfe *et al* (2000) found that parental understanding of there being no realistic chance of cure for their child came significantly later than the same belief in the physician. This delay had a negative impact on the quality of palliation that those children received. Wolfe *et al* acknowledge that in circumstances where a psychologist/social worker was involved in the care, the realisation came much earlier. In the West Midlands, where specialist nurses and social workers are routinely involved in all aspects of ongoing and palliative care, it seems that families are more likely to have good awareness of their child's disease progression.

A delicate balance exists between providing the family with support and guidance and continuing to enable them to feel in control. The challenge for the palliative care team is to ensure that families feel empowered and supported without being overwhelmed. Experienced practitioners will recognise the need to negotiate input with families – acknowledging that being at the forefront of care is not always necessary. It has been reported that involvement in care helps parents feel more in control and reduces their feelings of guilt (James and Johnson, 1997). The correct balance for one family will differ from that of another. Some families will require regular contact with professionals and input in every decision. Others will prefer to care for their child more independently. Specific advice, however, may be needed to give direction in decision-making, such as the management of new symptoms.

Key information from professional to family

There are key pieces of information that the palliative care team will need to convey to the family. The following are among the most important:

⌘ The disease is not considered by professionals to be curable. This does not necessarily equate with the family accepting that death is inevitable. Although parents should play a large part in the decision for curative treatment to be discontinued, it is important that they feel that the decision is made in partnership with the care team. Perceptions of isolation in their decision-making may contribute to families' subsequent feelings of guilt about their child's death or any suffering that he/she experienced.

⌘ The family can return to the treatment centre at any time for further consultations if required and professionals will be accessible to offer both support and symptom control.

⌘ Information on how to access professionals is essential. Showing families that any questions will be answered with honesty and respect is essential to the communication process.

⌘ How to ensure good symptom control and how to recognise the likely changes as death approaches.

⌘ What to do at the time of death and in the period immediately after. This includes: the consequences of dialling 999; that there is no time pressure on having the death confirmed by a GP; the options for where the child's body is kept; and how it should be cared for between the death and the funeral (see *Chapter 6*).

For many families, consideration of all the above issues at one time is not feasible; more often than not, these topics will be addressed over a series of meetings.

Many topics that need to be addressed can be very painful for family members. Non-verbal cues provide the practitioner with clues as to whether a family member is ready to have such a dialogue. This point is illustrated in *Case study 4.1*.

Case study 4.1

David was four years old and had incurable leukaemia. As David's health deteriorated, the family's Macmillan nurse tried repeatedly to engage Joy, his mother, in discussion about David's symptoms and imminent death. Her attempts were met with withdrawal of eye contact and a closing of Joy's physical posture. This gave a strong message that Joy was unwilling to discuss these matters. In time, the Macmillan nurse asked Joy when would be a good time to give her some important pieces of information. Joy said the Macmillan nurse should speak to David's uncle. The uncle was able to communicate that the family would prefer David to die in hospital.

As in this example, most families can identify at least one family member who is willing to acknowledge the reality of the situation, and feels able to discuss what should be done at the time of death. On the rare occasions when no family member has been able to accept the palliative nature of the disease process, the team have alerted local ambulance services and casualty departments to the situation.

It is helpful if, through verbal and non-verbal means, the healthcare professional can convey that:

- the family's suffering is recognised
- their uniqueness is appreciated
- the family's strengths, abilities and choices are respected
- possible feelings of guilt, anger, helplessness and hopelessness are recognised.

Key information from family to professionals

A twenty-four-hour presence at the family's home cannot be sustained by community services, nor would this be desired by the vast majority of families. This inevitably means that much symptom management will rely on parental reporting of the child's condition, often over the telephone. It is important that both parents and professionals have confidence that information about the child's condition is accurately relayed. Various strategies enable parents to report more precisely on their child's condition and consequently help them retain confidence and control:

- ⌘ Asking parents to keep written records of key events, such as new symptoms. The provision of charts, such as medication tick charts, will not only help professionals to establish what is happening in the home, but may also aid communication between different caregivers within the family.
- ⌘ The use of pain assessment tools or charts designed especially to assess a particular symptom (eg. a chart designed for recording the length, timing and nature of seizures). These ensure that symptoms can be more objectively quantified. As shown in *Case study 4.2*, this minimises the chances that parental perception will colour what the child reports.
- ⌘ Guiding parents by direct questioning through a full assessment of their child and his/her symptoms. *Case study 4.3* demonstrates that failure to ask a full range of questions can result in inappropriate advice and action.

Case study 4.2

Jason was fifteen years old and dying of leukaemia. Jason's parents were very accepting when the palliative phase began. The family had always been undemanding, and during the palliative phase the primary health care team became concerned that they were not contacted when Jason's pain was uncontrolled. Following a suggestion from a colleague, the family's district nurse spent time explaining to the family that, with correct intervention, the team expected to be able to keep Jason largely pain free. The family were asked to report pain scores over 2 on the 0–10 pain assessment tool that Jason was using. During the discussion it transpired that Jason's mother had witnessed a very traumatic death during Jason's inpatient treatment and had therefore believed that dying would inevitably be painful.

Case study 4.3

Mr Khalid contacted the on-call Macmillan nurse during the early hours of the morning in obvious distress. He reported that his son Mohammed was in great pain. Mr Khalid had given Mohammed his usual dose of sustained-release morphine some hours earlier. The Macmillan nurse therefore instructed him to give the breakthrough dose of morphine. When the father reported that the medication was trickling out of his son's mouth, the Macmillan nurse realised that the description of Mohammed was untypical of a child in pain. At this point the Macmillan nurse asked Mr Khalid to describe exactly what his son was doing, and from this was able to ascertain that Mohammed was having a seizure. She then instructed Mr Khalid how to treat this appropriately.

Communication — parent to parent

In the team's experience, the routine practice of giving both parents difficult news together supports honesty and good communication. However, it is recognised that men and women often adopt different coping strategies, which can make the sharing of grief problematic (Staudacher, 1991). Parents may try to protect each other or hide their concerns and feelings from one another. Thoughts of a gruesome death, a guilty desire for death to come quickly, concerns about funeral plans, or other issues that they perceive will add to the other's psychological burden may be unspoken. Parents may also misinterpret their partner's response to stress, with reluctance to verbalise thoughts perceived as unsupportive or uncaring. Communication may consequently break down. Helping parents to understand that their feelings are normal can be beneficial. If a parent can verbalise difficult thoughts to a third party, they may then be willing to consider that a partner might have similar concerns or to acknowledge to each other that they are using different coping strategies.

Guiding parents as partners through their child's palliation can be problematic. Couples may have been experiencing problems in their relationship before their child's diagnosis. For some, the burden of maintaining a relationship and the stress of their child's death is too great. Indeed, some relationships do not survive the death and bereavement period (Sarnoff Schiff, 1977).

Talking with children

Key information for children

⌘ Cancer is nobody's fault.
⌘ Cancer cannot be caused by thoughts or by bad behaviour.
⌘ Cancer is not 'catching'.
⌘ Cancer very rarely runs in families.

The development of a child's understanding of death (described in *Table 4.1, pp. 48–49*) has traditionally been thought to closely follow Piaget's stages of cognitive development (Piaget, 1969). It is, however, important to realise that children are often able to understand a more 'advanced' explanation than their years might suggest (Eiser, 1990).

Children have the right to information about their illness and the right to express their views on proposed treatments: these views should be given due weight (United Nations, 1989). However, like adults, children often use a range of coping mechanisms to help them deal with what is happening. Denial is widely used to avoid talking about what they cannot face, and it is known that not all children want to know full details about their illness (Young *et al*, 2003). For those attempting to communicate with the dying child, the key is to show a willingness to talk openly with the child, giving the child the control in deciding what he/she feels able to share. As part of the illness experience, many children will have learnt the taboos of disease and death. Skill and patience alongside a private and calm environment may therefore be required in order for the child to feel able to talk about these things.

Table 4.1: Development of a child's understanding of death

	Children's understanding of illness & death	Implications for the sick child	Implications for siblings
Infants and toddlers	Infants and toddlers have no concept of death, but are distressed by loss. Infants become skilled at interpreting non-verbal cues and will therefore rapidly recognise and be distressed by anxiety or upset in their care givers. They need frequent physical contact, interaction with parents and normal routines.	The sick child is more likely to be upset by the consequences of the illness, (eg. observing distress in their care givers, separation from loved ones, changes in their normal routine or frightening medical interventions) than by fear of impending death (Whaley and Wong, 1991).	For the very young sibling, parental absence, or their distraction when present, presents the biggest threat to the sibling's wellbeing. Palliative care at home has been shown to increase intimacy and communication, thereby enhancing a sibling's coping (Lauer et al, 1985). For children of this age, the inability to see the world from any perspective other than their own (egocentricity) mean that they do not comprehend the permanence of death and will need this to be explained repeatedly.
Pre-school child	The pre-school child remains egocentric, and as a result may see illness as a punishment. Death is seen as temporary and reversible. Care must be taken in explaining things to this age group as language is taken literally.	Being separated from care givers will be what the sick child fears from death. They will need constant reassurance that care givers will not leave them, that the illness is not a punishment and that those around them love and care for them (Brown, 1999). The opportunity to relay their level of pain or distress and to express fears or concerns may be effected through play, drawings or stories. The successful use of such tools, however, depends largely on the care givers' listening and observation abilities, and their skill in not over-interpreting or pre-empting the message that the child's activities convey.	Siblings may see themselves as responsible for the sick child's illness and death. Observing a parent's depression or withdrawal is likely to confirm their belief in their own guilt. When hearing that the sick child has gone and will not return, the sibling may fear that their parents too will not come back (Whaley and Wong, 1991). Children of this age have few defence mechanisms and often rely on denial to protect them from such a significant loss. This can be distressing for adult observers, who misinterpret the young child's attempts to distract themselves as a lack of concern.

Table 4.1 (cont'd): Development of a child's understanding of death

	Children's understanding of illness & death	Implications for the sick child	Implications for siblings
Schoolchild	School-aged children may still fear that bad behaviour has led to the illness, but with clear explanation these misconceptions are more easily dispelled than in younger children. At this stage, children know that some illnesses may be inherited or contagious, therefore a more detailed discussion on causality will be required. By the age of approximately 10 years there is a comprehension that death is inevitable, universal and permanent. Younger school-age children will, however, continue to need these concepts clarified repeatedly.	An increased cognitive capacity means that sick children of this age group fear the process of dying and death itself. Without explanation, children resort to fantasy, which can evoke more frightening images than the truth. Information and, where possible, choices help children to retain control and maintain a sense of self-worth. Opportunities to express emotions and discuss concerns, and reassurance of the love of their family and peers, are needed.	The concentration of adults' attention on the sick child frequently leads to feelings of jealousy, rejection and anger in siblings (Sargent *et al*, 1995). Guilt at such emotions often prevents siblings from telling adults how they feel. Reassurance that parents do sti~~ll~~ ~~lov~~e them and that they would get the same at~~tention if~~ they were sick is needed. Schoolchil~~dren need~~ factual information about what happ~~ens during~~ the time of death and during the proce~~sses and rituals~~ that follow. Children will use their imagi~~nations to fill~~ any gaps in their knowledge. Their fantasies are usually worse than the reality, so to give a child the option of being present at the death and the ceremonies that follow is likely to enhance their coping (Lauer *et al*, 1985)
Adolescent	Most adolescents have a mature understanding of death and many become interested in theological explanations.	The normal adolescent battle to be accepted by peers, and independent from parents, is thwarted by illness and treatment. At a time when adolescents are just establishing their place in the world, the threat of leaving it is unacceptable. The need to retain some independence and autonomy is strong, and the young adult is likely to value support from peers more than that from parents (see *Chapter 7*).	In adolescence, the grief of losing a sibling may manifest itself by withdrawal and an inability to express feelings in a direct manner. Some, however, are able to find trusted individuals with whom they can share some or all of the multiple emotions their grief brings.

Children's awareness

Children who are not told of the life-limiting nature of their illness will often have an awareness of what the future holds through their own experiences and the experiences of those around them. Bluebond-Langner (1989) described the stages through which children move in reaching an understanding that they are likely to die. From viewing themselves as a 'sick child', an understanding of treatments and their links with recovery develops. As the disease progresses the child begins to feel different from other children, and later believes that he/she will always be ill. Finally, there is a realisation that there are only a limited number of treatments available, which in turn leads to a direct or indirect understanding that death will follow. Lansdown (1988) summarises these steps in understanding as:

- I am very sick
- I have an illness that can kill people
- I have an illness that can kill children
- I may not get better
- I am dying.

Nitschke *et al* (1982) developed and used a 'final-stage conference' with children whose disease was not considered curable. This was a semi-structured interview with the child and parent(s) where children were told of their short prognosis and asked to decide whether or not to enter a phase II trial (see *Chapter 3*). The great majority of children made a decision about trial entry either autonomously or together with their family. Most of those choosing only palliative care tolerated the knowledge of their impending death well, and the authors felt that there was evidence that this approach enabled children to share their fears with their families.

Helping parents to communicate with their sick child

Many parents feel that they will be unable to talk to their child of his/her impending death. It is, however, important to encourage parents to:

- be open to signs that their child requires more information
- foster honesty
- take their cues from their child
- realise that what the child fears from death will differ from adults' fears
- consider the emotional cost of keeping the secret.

A child who says 'I don't know what is happening to me' is displaying fears and should be encouraged to expand on these worries. Conversely, children who change the subject whenever asked how they feel about their illness may be saying that they do not want further information. Care must be taken, as children will carefully choose with whom they feel comfortable discussing such sensitive issues. Older children may be wary of adding to their parents' fears, and hence only express their personal concerns to friends or professionals. Children who realise that things are being hidden from them may be similarly secretive about their thoughts and fears, and lose trust in those around them, which will, in turn, increase their fearfulness. They may also fear that the truth is so awful that it cannot be discussed. Some parents may be able to ask their child what they want to know, asking 'Would you want us to tell you if your leukaemia got worse?' A family may be able to address a child's fears about dying (i.e. by giving reassurance that the child will not be left alone, will have no more invasive medical procedures and will always be loved), even if they are not able to directly speak of death (Bodkin C, 2002, personal communication, Birmingham).

Parents may be helped to recognise the enormous strain that they are under in having to keep up a pretence, and the negative impact that the collusion has on their relationship with their sick child. Relatively few families manage full openness. In one study (Goldman and Christie, 1993), only 19% of families mutually acknowledged the impending death with their sick child, and even fewer — only 3% — openly discussed the death. In this study a similar number of children were felt to know of the impending death but chose not to discuss it. More worryingly, a small number of children were blocked by parents if they talked about the situation. However, parents in this study did find it easier to talk to the sick child's siblings: 75% managed to tell them of the impending death.

Allowing open communication with a very sick child can be frightening. Family members and professionals alike may fear the question 'Am I going to die?' It is important to try to confirm what information the child seeks and to establish their current level of knowledge. To respond with questions such as 'Have you been worrying that you are dying?' and 'What makes you think that?' will allow the child to expand upon his/her fears and ensure that the right question is answered. Children may merely need reassurance that they are not expected to die imminently. Children who have the strength to ask such questions usually want to discuss the issue, and have the capacity, with support, to cope with the answer.

If open communication is established, children may want to discuss issues such as how death might be, what happens afterwards, fears of punishment for wrongdoings and whether parents will be all right. It is important for them to know that they will always be loved and remembered, and to have a sense of the lasting impact of the life they have led. For some children, as illustrated in *Case study 4.4*, this will involve 'putting things in order' by visiting people and places that are important to them or deciding who should receive treasured possessions.

Case study 4.4

Kelly, aged fifteen, knew that she was dying. She decided to plan the last few months of her life. Her ambition had been to become a teacher. Unable to complete coursework for her GCSEs, Kelly chose to spend time as a voluntary classroom assistant in her local primary school. She made a will and wrote letters to significant people in her life, thanking them for their support and kindness. These were stored away until after her death. Finally, Kelly planned her funeral, choosing the songs and readings. After her death, Kelly's family gained comfort from the knowledge that she was able to have some control over her last few months of life. They were able to freely discuss death with her and her plans to 'keep a close eye on them from heaven!'

Even children who appear to have a full knowledge of their prognosis will seem to fluctuate in their awareness, at times making unrealistic plans for the future. Young people are known to be able to hold two such concepts simultaneously, and this in itself does not indicate that they are unaware of the reality of the situation (Lansdown, 1988). In fact, to challenge such dreams may deny the child hope.

Direct discussion around death and dying may prove too threatening for the child. Through the experience of organising support weekends for siblings of cancer patients, the Birmingham Children's Hospital Oncology Unit and WMPMT have noted that children and young people seem more comfortable expressing their feelings when the focus is an activity, eg. creation of a newsletter or board game, rather than directly on the siblings themselves. In palliative care it is rare to have the opportunity for group activities with sick children or siblings, but other tools can provide an alternative focus.

Story books allow children to consider the emotions and coping mechanisms of others facing similar challenges. Encouraging a child to record their experiences and advice for others in the same position aids clarification of current events and feelings. It also helps children to recognise that they have found ways to cope effectively with very challenging circumstances. The therapeutic use of play requires specialist input. However, nurses can look for clues to children's understanding and feelings in their pictures and games. These clues can then be used to stimulate conversations addressing misconceptions and exploring feelings.

In her work with children dying of leukaemia, Bluebond-Langner (1980) revealed how children as young as three years often have an awareness of their impending death. Children's awareness of social taboos, however, will prevent them from openly discussing their awareness with those adults whom they feel cannot handle such discussion. More than twenty years on, it is not uncommon to find parents and children observing this mutual pretence: both parties knowing that death is inevitable while neither acknowledges this to the other.

If parents can be helped to recognise this, it may be possible to offer the child support and an opportunity to talk openly. This may involve direct professional input to the child or support for the parents in order that they may do so.

Adolescents

Adolescents present particular challenges. Teenage years are a period of great emotional and physical change, which often result in the adolescent feeling misunderstood. This may cause conflict within the family. A terminal illness in addition will sometimes mean that the relationship with parents deteriorates further. Friends may be missed (Claflin and Barbarin, 1991) but are often considered too pitying, afraid to discuss the issue or simply absent (Tebbi *et al*, 1985). Sometimes friends may be pushed away as the teenager considers himself unacceptably 'different'. In view of such isolation, it is easy to understand the anger or withdrawal that results.

As professionals at the receiving end of a teenager's rage it can be easy to retreat defensively. But for many healthy teenagers, withdrawal and anger are part of growing up. For adolescents with incurable disease, the injustice of their imminent death is likely to compound these feelings and can provoke a plethora of problems. The balance between respecting the young person's privacy and showing availability and willingness to talk is challenging. (Issues concerning adolescents are discussed in depth in *Chapter 7*.)

Siblings

Life as a sibling of a child undergoing cancer treatment is known to be stressful. In the largest study of the impact on healthy children of their siblings' apparently successful cancer treatment (Sahler *et al*, 1994), a doubling of the incidence of emotional or behavioural problems was found to have resulted from the experience. The additional psychological impact of the sick child's death at the end of this experience leaves some children with considerable behavioural and emotional difficulties, far exceeding the incidence found in normal populations (Pettle Michael and Lansdown, 1986).

Other cultures

Care is needed in communication with families from other cultures. Some families may have the additional burden of a language barrier. Furthermore, in some ethnic groups, offering the child control through information and involvement in their treatment may not be seen as beneficial. In some cultures, such as Latin American and some Asian cultures, children are expected to be more submissive and follow the decisions of their elders (Die Trill and Kovalcik, 1997). In other cultures, such as Southern European, the custom of 'non-disclosure' would clearly impact on professional openness. Likewise, it is the cultural norm for the Chinese not to discuss death and dying for fear of summoning bad luck (Stevens, 1995).

Assumptions should not be made about a certain group's beliefs; rather, a full assessment should be carried out of that family's individual views. Ideally this should be in the family's own language, and should elicit their views on the disease, treatment, communication within the family and what help would be welcomed from health professionals (Die Trill and Kovalcik, 1997).

Talking with schools

A dying child has the same need for stimulation and development as a child with a normal life expectancy. School provides contact with peers, an opportunity to achieve, and a degree of normality. For many children, school is a place where they love to be: in one study (Bouffet *et al*, 1997), 60% of children with incurable malignancy were shown to have a desire to attend school until an advanced stage of their illness, with some of these children exhibiting an almost desperate desire to learn.

From the school's point of view, the presence of a terminally ill pupil in the classroom will bring a host of emotional and practical challenges. The challenge of meeting the needs of a sick child while preparing their peers and teachers for the impending death can make this a very stressful period for the school. Advice and support from specialist healthcare professionals can be valuable during the child's attendance at school and around the time of ,and subsequent to, the death of the child.

Open and honest communication is advocated, but this decision ultimately rests with the parents. Full openness within the school from the start of palliation may be neither possible nor desirable for a variety of reasons. Where a sick child or siblings do not try to have full knowledge of the situation, it will be necessary to ensure that other pupils do not know more.

School is often the cornerstone of the child and siblings' community and may also encompass links to parents' social network. Parents may wish to avoid having to deal with well-meaning remarks and questioning looks when collecting their children from school. While the wider community of the school remains oblivious, it is easier for the child and siblings, at some level, or at certain times, to 'deny' what is happening by escaping into the normality of the school environment.

In many cases, a child will have been attending school during curative treatment; staff will therefore have developed strategies for dealing with issues such as hair loss, protection from infection and fatigue. If the illness is new or has not been discussed recently in the school, ideally the child's peer group should be told some basic facts about cancer (See 'Key information for children', earlier in this chapter).

In addition, teachers will benefit from knowing:

- sick children's level of knowledge about their disease
- that most children deteriorate gradually and dramatic changes in the classroom are very unlikely
- how to manage anticipated symptoms
- how to contact parents and professionals.

The dying child may be more willing to share his/her feelings with, and ask questions of, trusted school staff than family members. It is important that the school is aware of the family's religious beliefs and whether the family will allow staff to answer questions honestly. Attendance may need to be carefully planned around the child's energy levels. Research suggests that terminally ill children tend to want to focus on developing skills in a very limited number of subjects (Bouffet *et al,* 1997).

Most teachers find teaching a terminally ill child very distressing, and express particular difficulty in knowing how to manage the rest of the class (Bouffet *et al,* 1997). Many teachers imparting information about the disease and impending death fear that they will show their own distress in front of the class. Teachers can be reassured that their own emotional expression not only shows they care, but can also allow them to become role models, giving pupils permission to express how they are feeling.

Teachers should know:

- that their unique relationship with the child is acknowledged
- that their own reactions of shock, disbelief, anger and sadness at the news of a child's imminent death are normal
- that support is available for teaching staff who may feel ill-prepared to meet the challenges of supporting the child, family and fellow pupils
- how to impart information to the child's peers, answer questions, and deal with their grief.

As the child deteriorates, pupils will need further information and should be told that the child is very ill and that there is concern that he/she may die. It is hoped that this will be part of ongoing discussions where pupils feel able to ask questions and receive honest answers.

Case study 4.5

Miss Jennings sat the class of six- and seven-year-olds on the carpet at the front of the classroom. She said that she had something very sad to tell them. She explained that Marcus's leukaemia had come back and that the doctors had tried their very best but had not been able to make it go away. She told them that Marcus had died that morning and that he was now not feeling ill anymore. She told the class that she believed that Marcus was now in heaven with God, who would look after him very well. Having already sought permission from Marcus's family, the school sent a letter to all parents informing them of Marcus's death and outlining how to support their children in their grief.

Over the following weeks the class asked many questions about the nature of the illness, the death and heaven. Miss Jennings was supported by the deputy head, the parish priest and the community children's nurse in encouraging the class to express their feelings. Over the following weeks the class wrote a book of their memories of Marcus which they gave to his family. Six months later, on Marcus's birthday, the school held a ceremony to dedicate a playground bench in memory of Marcus.

Like the school in *Case study 4.5*, many schools are able to find a way to make lasting tributes to the child that has died. Although families often find attendance at memorial events very distressing, such tributes are greatly appreciated in the longer term as a sign that the deceased child will not be forgotten.

Talking among professionals

During their child's treatment, the family will meet many people from the multidisciplinary team. In the palliative care phase it is preferable to minimise this number if possible. Continuity of care remains the focus. Collaboration between the professionals involved ensures that the child and family receive the appropriate input from the essential disciplines. For a multidisciplinary approach to be effective, it is necessary for guidelines to be established from the outset. Each professional caring for the child during palliation subscribes to membership of a new, often 'virtual' team where common goals of palliation and mutual support are implicit, even though all team members do not necessarily physically meet.

It is important that the multiprofessional team establishes good pathways of communication for disseminating information about treatment plans and updates on the child's condition and needs. This process is often facilitated by a primary health care team meeting. Each professional must respect the unique and vital role of the other disciplines involved. Professionals within a discipline (eg. community nurses) should have a team approach to care, to ensure that ongoing cover is provided and that no team member becomes 'burnt out' (see *Chapter 8*). In large teams, the allocation of a 'named' or 'primary' nurse may be beneficial. Professionals from disciplines where an individual member of a team is involved (eg. community physiotherapist) will need to recognise their own professional and emotional limitations and have access to support from colleagues.

Good communication between professionals will result in families receiving consistent information. This in turn will give parents confidence in the organisation of care and the skill of the team caring for their child.

Summary

Each child and family is unique, and will therefore have a unique set of needs and coping strategies. Although relevant experience is invaluable, even a veteran professional will continue to encounter new challenges. Professionals inevitably make mistakes in their attempts to communicate effectively. By facing up to these errors and expressing regret at the distress caused, they should be able to rescue most relationships. It is far better for professionals to show a true desire to learn from the unique experiences of a family than to allow the fear of a blunder to stop them reaching out to a family.

References

Bluebond-Langner M (1980) *The Private Worlds of Dying Children*. Princeton University Press, Princeton

Bluebond-Langner M (1989) Worlds of dying children and their well siblings. *Death Stud* **13**: 1–16

Bouffet E, Zuchinelli V, Costanzo P (1997) Schooling as part of palliative care in paediatric oncology. *Palliat Med* **11**: 133–9

Brown E. (1999) 'Loss, change and grief: working with life-limited and life-threatened children'. The Acorn's Lecture. Acorn's Children's Hospice, Birmingham

Claflin J, Barbarin OA (1990) Does 'Telling' less protect more? Relationships among age, information disclosure, and what children with cancer see and feel. *J Pediatr Psychol* **16**(2): 169–91

Die Trill M, Kovalcik R (1997) The child with cancer: influence of culture on truth-telling and patient care. *Ann N Y Acad Sci* **809**: 197–210

Eiser C (1990) *Chronic Childhood Disease: An introduction to psychology theory and research*. Cambridge University Press, Cambridge

Goldman A, Christie D (1993) Children with cancer talk about their own death with their families. *Pediatr Hematol Oncol* **10**(3): 223–31

James L, Johnson B (1997) The needs of parents of pediatric oncology patients during the palliative care phase. *J Pediatr Oncol Nurs* **14**(2): 83–95

Lansdown R (1988) Communicating with children. In: Goldman A (Ed). *Care of the Dying Child*. Oxford University Press, Oxford

Lauer M, Mulhern R, Bohne J, Camitta BM (1985) Children's perceptions of their sibling's death at home or hospital: the precursors of differential adjustment. *Cancer Nurs* **8**: 21–7

Lloyd-Williams M (2002) Breaking bad news to patients and relatives. *Br Med J Career Focus* **325**: S11

Nitschke R, Humphrey GB, Sexauer CL *et al* (1982) Therapeutic choices made by patients with end-stage cancer. *J Pediatr* **101**(3): 471–6

Pettle Michael SA, Lansdown RG (1986) Adjustment to the death of a sibling. *Arch Dis Child* **61**: 278–83

Piaget J (1969) *The Theory of Stages in Cognitive Development*. McGraw Hill Book Company, NewYork

Sahler OJ, Roghmann KJ, Carpenter PJ *et al* (1994) Sibling adaptation to childhood cancer collaborative study: prevalence of sibling distress and definition of adaptation levels. *J Dev Behav Pediatr* **15**(5): 353–66

Sargent JR, Sahler OJ, Roghmann KJ *et al* (1995) Sibling adaptation to childhood cancer collaborative study: siblings' perceptions of the cancer experience. *J Pediatr Psychol* **20**(2): 151–64

Sarnoff Schiff H (1977) *The Bereaved Parent*. Penguin Books, New York

Staudacher C (1991) *Men and Grief: A guide for men surviving the death of a loved one. A resource for caregivers and mental health professionals*. New Harbinger Publications, Oaklands CA

Stevens M, O'Riordan E (1996) Family responses when a child with cancer is palliative. *J Palliat Care* **12**(3): 51–5

Stevens MM (1995) Family adjustment and support. In: Doyle D, Hanks G, MacDonald N (Eds). *Oxford Textbook of Palliative Medicine*. Oxford University Press, Oxford: 707–17

Tebbi CK, Stern M, Boyle M, Mettlin CJ, Mindell ER (1985) The role of social support systems in adolescent cancer amputees. *Cancer* **56**: 965–71

United Nations (1989) *Convention on the Rights of the Child. Articles 12 and 13*. United Nations, Geneva.

Whaley LF, Wong DL (1991) *Nursing Care of Infants and Children*. 4th edn. Mosby-Year Book, St Louis

Wolfe J, Klar N, Grier HE *et al* (2000) Understanding of prognosis among parents of children who died of cancer: impact on treatment goals and integration of palliative care. *JAMA* **284**(19): 2469–75

Woolley H, Stein A, Forrest GC, Baum JD (1989) Imparting the diagnosis of life-threatening illness in children. *Br Med J* **293**: 1623–6

Young B, Dixon-Woods M, Windridge KC, Heney D (2003) Managing communication with young people who have a potentially life-threatening chronic illness: qualitative study of patients and parents. *Br Med J* **326**: 305

5

Symptom management

This chapter will discuss a range of symptoms and management strategies associated with paediatric palliative care. Although many of the symptoms will be prevalent in other diseases, the West Midland Paediatric Macmillan Team's (WMPMT's) experience is primarily in paediatric oncology and haematology. Care must therefore be taken when applying the principles elsewhere. For example, alterations in the drug doses and frequencies recommended in the symptom control and palliative care guidelines are likely to be necessary in the child with significant renal or hepatic disease.

This part of the book is divided into four sections:

Section A   Introduction to symptom control

Section B   Management of pain

Section C   Management of symptoms other than pain

Section D   Symptom control and palliative care guidelines

Section A considers the principles of symptom management, limitations and practical aspects. **Section B** exclusively addresses pain management. **Section C** is subdivided into specific disease processes to facilitate a review of other common symptoms in paediatric palliative care. The titles of these are:

⌘ Bone marrow disease
⌘ Solid tumours including thoracic and abdominal disease
⌘ Central nervous system disease.

Each disease process is complemented by a case study that enables discussion of a range of associated symptoms. Where pharmacological interventions are indicated in Sections A, B and C, dose ranges are not suggested, but can be found in the symptom control and palliative care guidelines presented in **Section D**.

Section A

Introduction to symptom control

As a child's condition deteriorates, symptoms relating to the disease process and treatment are likely to manifest themselves. The range of symptoms may include many of those seen in adult haematology and oncology palliative care. Nevertheless, the input of a specialist paediatric practitioner will be required, for the following reasons:

⌘ The unique needs of the child and family (Association for Children with Life-Threatening or Terminal Conditions and Their Families [ACT] and the Royal College of Paediatrics and Child Health, 1997).
⌘ The need to administer drug doses and preparations that are not comparable to those used in adult care.
⌘ The need to administer drugs that are not licensed for use in in paediatrics.

The majority of children cared for by the WMPMT require opioid analgesia for pain control during the palliative care phase. Other common symptoms include nausea and vomiting, anorexia, fatigue and pruritus. Of equal importance and attributable to disease progression is loss of function, eg. dysphasia, ataxia and immobility. These symptoms require equally careful consideration and management. Pre-existing disease processes can also complicate symptom management, ie. patients with renal impairment may have difficulty in excreting drug metabolites. Children may also experience natural events that require age-appropriate responses, eg. period pain. These may be misdiagnosed as disease related, as the focus of care moves towards palliation.

Aids to symptom control

Assessment

Assessment is the foundation of good symptom management. History taking, listening and questioning are crucial to the process. Experienced practitioners will not take things at 'face value' — they will question the obvious and consider the whole picture. Likewise, perceptual awareness is fundamental to good nursing judgment (Benner, 1984). A gut instinct — a sense of uneasiness or feeling that something is wrong — is an emotion that expert nurses frequently describe when assessing patients. Although this approach has been criticised for its lack of analytical design (Farrington, 1993), the WMPMT acknowledge that an 'intuitive' grasp of a situation is a recognised phenomenon and should be considered within the assessment process.

Frequent reassessment must be undertaken, and documentation should be thorough. The child and family should be aware that their observations and reports of symptoms are considered essential in the assessment process. The experienced practitioner will consider them a vital resource in the child's symptom management (Carter, 1994).

Young children may not have the verbal or cognitive ability to let carers know about their symptoms. Changes in the child's behaviour may therefore be the best or only indicator. Assessment will consequently rely heavily on parental reporting. Reports should be treated seriously, even if the cause is not readily apparent. Parents express great frustration and guilt when professionals are unwilling to give credence to their findings (Ferrell *et al,* 1994).

Assessment tools

Children's varying cognitive and verbal skills can make their ability to describe, and hence understand, their symptoms difficult. It has, however, been demonstrated that even very young children are able to communicate their pain if an appropriate assessment tool is used (Ross and Ross, 1984).

Establishing the severity of symptoms can be particularly challenging. The use of assessment tools can allow children to quantify their symptoms and provide an objective assessment of the baseline severity and the efficacy of any intervention used. Most assessment tools were designed primarily for pain assessment, but can be adapted to assess a child's perception of other symptoms, such as nausea, anxiety and breathlessness. However, in the palliative phase, multiple symptoms often occur simultaneously and interact, making both measurement and control of symptoms complex (Lenz *et al,* 1997).

If the child has previously used an assessment tool effectively, it is appropriate to continue using it. Switching between alternative tools should be avoided unless there is a defined need. Below are some examples of assessment tools used by the WMPMT.

⌘ **Wong–Baker Faces scale** (Wong and Baker,1988): With this tool the child is able to report pain using cartoon faces that range from a happy face, indicating no pain, through to a crying and miserable face, indicating severe pain (*Figure 5.1*). By adapting the explanation given to the child, this tool could be used for the assessment of other symptoms, as no written language is used. Experience has shown, however, that children can misinterpret the scale. One child would not rate his pain at the maximum level, despite apparently experiencing severe pain. When questioned, he explained that this was because the child in the drawing was crying and he was not.

0	1	2	3	4	5
No hurt	Hurts little bit	Hurts little more	Hurts even more	Hurts whole lot	Hurts worst

Figure 5.1: Wong–Baker FACES Pain Rating Scale (Wong and Baker, 1988). From Wong DL, Hockenberry-Eaton M, Wilson D, Winkelstein ML, Schwartz P: *Wong's Essentials of Pediatric Nursing*, 6/e, St Louis, 2001, p. 1301. Copyrighted by Mosby, Inc. Reprinted by permission

⌘ **Personal diaries**: Personal diaries can provide useful information in the assessment of symptoms by outlining episodes, site and duration. The format of the diary can be constructed in collaboration with the child, and be personalised in keeping with their age. Either the child or the parent can complete the diary.

⌘ **Eland colour scale** (Eland, 1988): This tool not only provides information concerning the severity of pain, but also allows the child to pinpoint the pain sites through the use of an outline figure (*Figure 5.2*). Coloured crayons should accompany this tool to enable the child to nominate a colour for each type of pain. The child then marks the diagram with the appropriate colour at the site or sites of pain. This is a useful tool for multi-site pain, which is often difficult to assess.

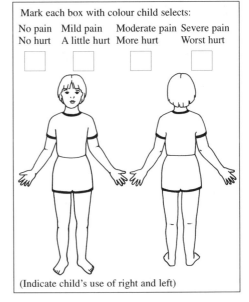

Mark each box with colour child selects:

No pain	Mild pain	Moderate pain	Severe pain
No hurt	A little hurt	More hurt	Worst hurt

(Indicate child's use of right and left)

Figure 5.2: Eland colour scale (Eland, 1988)

Both the personal diaries and the Eland colour scale require time and energy to complete. The very sick child may therefore not be able to do use these.

Family education and preparation

Warning families about impending symptoms can often increase their confidence (Beardsmore and Alder, 1994). While it may be considered upsetting to discuss particularly alarming symptoms if they are not a certainty, it can be more traumatic to have omitted information about such potential problems if they then occur. An unanticipated seizure, for example, can be very frightening for the family. Experience has shown that families who have been taught to recognise such symptoms and who have an appropriate action plan feel more in control (Beardsmore and Fitzmaurice, 2002). Families rarely recoil from learning to administer medication via alternative routes, eg. rectally. The benefits of being able to take control and do something to alleviate their child's distress appear to outweigh parental fears.

Open communication

Children who do not understand what is happening to them are more likely to be frightened by the disease process. Fear increases the respiratory rate, exacerbating breathlessness and causes muscle tension, worsening pain. Children who detect the conspiracy of silence may feel unable to express their true concerns. The distress may then be exhibited as symptoms that prove difficult to control.

Children should, wherever possible, be given the opportunity to talk through their understanding of the disease and any fears. In families where there is little communication, the child may be reassured to know that further traumatic treatments are not planned and that he/she will not be left alone, even if the poor prognosis cannot be directly addressed.

Methodological approach

A systematic approach to symptom management is essential. The use of techniques such as spinal analgesia, nerve block or even alternative opioids should be avoided before exhaustive manipulation of conventional therapies. Failure to utilise basic measures to counteract symptoms before employing more sophisticated techniques can give rise to subsequent questioning of the role of the neglected component. This is of particular concern if the symptoms continue uncontrolled. Likewise, overprescribing should be avoided. The administration of an excessive number of drugs in paediatric symptom management is likely to result in failed overall compliance, including essential analgesia. Careful weighing of the benefits against the costs of adjuvant medication is required, and constant review should be the gold standard practice.

Multidisciplinary approach

Symptom control is most successfully delivered using a multidisciplinary approach in which healthcare professionals are able to seek advice from colleagues. Team meetings should include both nursing and medical staff. The WMPMT also liases closely with other key professionals, including a pharmacist, physiotherapists, occupational therapists, dietitians and speech therapists.

Early in palliation, it is usual for a primary care team meeting to be held, and this is followed by regular contact between these professionals (see *Chapter 2*). At Birmingham Children's Hospital, the team holds a weekly palliative care meeting. At each meeting the child and family are discussed in relation to their physical, psychosocial and spiritual wellbeing. Management strategies are debated and decisions challenged. Current and emerging innovations from the available literature and personal contacts are shared. Both ward staff and visiting professionals from related disciplines are encouraged to join the meeting and contribute. It is also a valuable forum for supporting staff (see *Chapter 8*).

Equipment and protocols

A number of initiatives have enabled the WMPMT to deliver symptom control more effectively within the community setting.

Palliative care equipment cases

Several recurring problems led to the realisation that the provision of symptom control for children dying of a malignancy within the West Midlands could be improved (Fitzmaurice *et al*, 1997):

⌘ The often rapidly changing symptoms of the child, necessitating new drugs or methods of administration.

⌘ The difficulty in accessibility and availability of drugs, particularly 'out of hours'.

⌘ The large geographical area covered by the WMPMT.

An informal approach had previously been adopted; this relied on the individual nurse's skills in anticipating the changing needs of the dying child and acquiring the necessary drugs and equipment.

In order to standardise the approach, the WMPMT worked together with the pharmacy department at Birmingham Children's Hospital to develop palliative care equipment cases containing the most commonly required intravenous and rectal drugs, along with equipment most likely to be needed to set up a syringe driver in the home.

The case contains all the necessary equipment to commence an infusion via the central venous line, Vascuport or subcutaneous route. The WMPMT routinely use a Graseby MS26 pump for infusions. As the child's condition deteriorates, the case and the reason why it may prove useful to the child's nursing care are discussed with the family. With the agreement of the primary health care team, the paediatric Macmillan nurse will deliver the case to the child's home. Storing the case within the child's home enables the GP to prescribe medication in the knowledge that the drugs and necessary equipment are easily accessible and ready for immediate administration.

Senior members of the medical staff at Birmingham Children's Hospital authorise the drugs contained in the case to be released from pharmacy. A prescription for a 'starting dose' of intravenous or subcutaneous drugs to match the child's anticipated symptom progression is also included. The prescription usually contains relevant doses of diamorphine and cyclizine, along with a sedative if this is thought to be necessary. A sheet with recommended doses for other drugs contained in the case is also included. Where possible, subsequent prescriptions are then negotiated with the child's general practitioner.

Symptom control and palliative care guidelines

The WMPMT, together with the pharmacy department and paediatric oncologist, has produced guidelines for symptom management — *Symptom Control and Palliative Care in Children with Cancer* (see *Section D*). These guidelines offer a general approach to the overall management of children dying of a malignancy. The emphasis is on drug doses and regimens, but there is also a section on a non-pharmacological approach to care not detailed in this book. When a child moves into the palliative phase of care, the guidelines are circulated to the multidisciplinary community team.

Both the palliative care equipment cases and the guidelines form an important part of the overall organisation and management of children dying from malignancy at home in the West Midlands.

Accessibility of specialist services

It is considered best practice for the paediatric outreach team to provide twenty-four-hour access for specialist advice and information, thus enhancing the input of the primary health care team (ACT and RCPCH, 1997). Within the West Midlands, the team provides a twenty-four-hour telephone on-call system. A substantial proportion of service time is allocated to the education and support of primary health care teams, enabling them to provide hands-on care. Round-the-clock access to a specialist nurse, along with the use of the palliative care guidelines and equipment case, allow local teams to provide this care with adequate support. The child and family also have direct access to the on-call Macmillan nurse.

In some parts of the UK, specialist practitioners offer a twenty-four-hour visiting on-call service to palliative patients. In general, this system is only feasible when the geographical area and population covered are small. Following attempts with a variety of systems in the West Midlands, it is felt that the benefits of having hands-on input from a specialist nurse out of hours are outweighed by the problems of the length of time the family must wait for the professional to arrive, often from a distant location, and the possible disempowerment of local professionals.

Limitations in symptom management

For a variety of reasons, there is limited research in paediatric palliative care (Cooley *et al,* 2000). The ethics of the use of randomised controlled trials to test the benefit of an intervention is questionable, since the number of patients is relatively small and consent for such trials is fraught with difficulty. Ideally, one would obtain consent from both parents and child. Informed consent involves much more than giving permission (Brookes, 2000). To give informed consent, the child would need to be fully conversant with his/her situation. The competence of the child to give consent would need to be considered and assessed (Jeffrey, 1993). There is also the potential for disagreement between the child and family about the best way forward.

Research evidence can, however, be gleaned from allied specialties, although care must be taken in generalising the results to the paediatric palliative care setting. As will be seen in later sections of this chapter, the findings of studies examining drug use in adult palliative care (Gourlay, 1998) and general paediatrics (Kart *et al*, 1997) can often provide pointers to appropriate practice in the child dying of cancer.

There is a lack of palliative care training for doctors at both undergraduate and postgraduate levels (Hilden *et al*, 2001), with a scarcity of information on palliative care in general medical textbooks (Quill and Billings, 1998). Often the anxiety of caring for a palliative patient is heightened on the relatively rare occasions when the patient is a child. In the UK, the founding of a special interest group of The Royal College of Paediatricians and Child Health is already proving an effective catalyst in the provision of 'best practice' and in the development of effective training programmes in paediatric palliative care (Goldman, 2001).

The Paediatric Oncology Outreach Nurses Group of the Royal College of Nursing provides the opportunity for nurses to share their experience and research findings with others involved in the palliation of children with malignancy. This group has, to date, not had the resources to undertake any large studies. Similarly, a special interest group for pharmacists with an interest in paediatric palliative care now exists.

Formal teaching programmes on the care of the child dying of cancer appear to be hard to find in any discipline, with many staff undertaking courses in other adult or paediatric specialties and studying paediatric palliation when the course allows.

Section B

Management of pain

Pain is one of the symptoms most commonly experienced by children dying of cancer (Wolfe *et al,* 2000). Parents fear pain more than any other symptom, and many have anxieties that it will not be controlled (Pursell, 1994). This section will consider the most effective ways to address pain in children with progressive malignancy. It will discuss pharmacological management (both opioid and non-opioid analgesia), as well as techniques for the non-pharmacological management of pain.

Pharmacological management

The World Health Organization analgesic ladder (WHO, 1998) is considered the gold standard in adult palliation, and is also applicable within the paediatric palliative care setting (*Figure 5.3*)

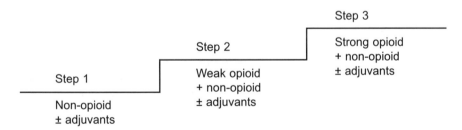

Figure 5.3: World Health Organization analgesic ladder

The administration of analgesia should be regular (by the clock) rather than as required, and, wherever possible, via the oral route (WHO, 1998). Frequent evaluation of the efficacy of the regimen is needed. Progression to the next step on the ladder is indicated when the maximum dose has been reached and pain remains unresolved, as an alternative analgesic of a comparable strength will not be effective. Although a variety of drugs can be utilised on each step of the ladder, regular use of a small number prevents confusion.

Although progression through the ladder should normally be stepwise, should assessment indicate the need to do so, a step in the ladder can be omitted in order to achieve symptom control.

Non-opioid analgesia

Consistent with the WHO analgesic ladder, non-opioids should be used as first-line treatment in the management of pain. Drugs in this category include paracetamol and non-steroidal anti-inflammatory drugs (NSAIDs). Paracetamol has a low incidence of side-effects, whereas NSAIDs can be effective when inflammation contributes to pain.

NSAIDs such as ibuprofen and diclofenac sodium have documented side-effects, which include inhibition of platelet function and gastrointestinal upset, both of which can be problematic. Despite usual avoidance of NSAIDS in children with bone marrow failure, the WMPMT have occasionally found it necessary to include them in the drug regimen of children with very low platelet counts. In these cases, their addition did not appear to be associated with exacerbation of bleeding problems. The newer NSAIDs, cyclo-oxygenase 2 (COX II) inhibitors (eg. celecoxib and rofecoxib), are thought to have fewer side-effects. To date they are not licensed in children, but evidence suggests that they are effective and incur less risk of bleeding and gastrointestinal disturbance (Bloom, 2001). Although the anti-inflammatory action of NSAIDs may not be fully effective for up to three weeks (*British National Formulary*, 47 March 2004), it is the experience of the team that patients gain benefit considerably earlier.

Paracetamol and NSAIDs have additional application as antipyretics. Fever may occur during palliation as a result of infection or the disease process. Paracetamol is the first-line antipyretic agent, with the addition of ibuprofen if paracetamol alone does not provide optimum relief.

Due to their different modes of action, paracetamol and NSAIDs can be used alongside opioids, either together or individually. Such combinations may be effective for pain that would not be fully controlled by an opiate alone (Tobias, 2000).

Aspirin is not recommended as an analgesic in children because of the risk of Reye's syndrome (Macdonald, 2002).

Weak opioids

A weak opioid, eg. codeine, should be introduced at the first sign that pain is not controlled by the non-opioid regimen. Part of the analgesic action of codeine is believed to be due to a proportion (2–10%) being metabolised to morphine in the body (Tywcross *et al*, 1998). Codeine also has a direct analgesic effect, but unlike strong opioids it does have a ceiling dose. Failure at optimal doses should therefore result in a rapid move to strong opioid medication. Switching between weak opioids is not recommended when pain is not controlled (Twycross and Wilcock, 2001). Constipation is a predictable side-effect of weak opioid administration and should be anticipated, allowing concurrent commencement of a laxative (see *Section C* of this chapter for further information).

Strong opioids

Morphine is the standard first-line strong opioid, with pharmacological data supporting its use in children. It must, however, be noted that babies up to two months of age will require less morphine per kilogram of body weight as neonates and infants metabolise morphine differently from older children and adults (Kart *et al*, 1997). The greatest benefit of this group of drugs is that, unlike non-opioids and weak opioids, they do not have a maximum dose beyond which a therapeutic effect is achieved.

Wherever possible, morphine should be given by mouth. Unrelieved pain is not an indication that a strong opioid should be administered parenterally (Regnard and Tempest, 1998) as oral morphine is just as likely to be effective as intravenous or subcutaneous morphine, provided that the child has normal absorption. Oral morphine is available in normal-release and slow-release preparations (see *Table 5.1*).

Table 5.1: Morphine preparations	
Short acting	**Long acting**
Tablets	Tablets
Suspension	Granules (suspension)*
Single-use vials	Rectal tampon**
Suppositories	

*When the prescribed dose requires a proportion of the dose included in the sachet, it has become common practice for a measured amount of water to be added to the sachet in order to attain the correct proportion, with the remaining preparation being discarded. Although the manufacturers do not advise this, and it is recognised that this may result in variable dosages being administered, experience shows that in practice this does not appear to be a problem.

**The modified-release rectal morphine Moraxen (Davis, 2000) has limited use in paediatrics because of the need to remove the suppository after twenty-four hours.

When commencing morphine it is considered best practice to establish requirements using normal-release preparations (Hanks *et al,* 2001). Once the therapeutic dose has been established, transfer to the sustained-release preparation is undertaken and the normal-release preparation is used for breakthrough pain. In practice, however, the team has found it possible to move successfully directly to a sustained-release preparation. Careful assessment, appropriate use of breakthrough analgesia and progression through the analgesic ladder (WHO, 1998) are the key to achieving this. In adults it is recommended that when starting the patient on a modified-release preparation the dose should not be changed more frequently than once every forty-eight hours (Hanks *et al,* 2001). However, the WMPMT team has found that more frequent changes in dosage have proved safe and effective, eg. in children with rapidly progressing disease.

Whether normal- or modified-release preparations are used for regular doses, the family should be encouraged to give additional doses of normal-release morphine as needed to control any breakthrough pain the child may have. The dose of breakthrough medication should equate to one-sixth of the total daily dose.

If the child's pain has been poorly controlled and the child has required two or more doses of breakthrough medication during the previous twenty-four-hour period, the total daily dose should be increased. The amount and frequency of breakthrough medication required, combined with clinical assessment, will indicate the required increase. This is usually between 30% and 50%, with breakthrough doses being adjusted proportionally (see *Figure 5.4*).

Case study 5.1

Selina, aged six, had progressive rhabdomyosarcoma. For the past two months she had been experiencing increasing pain requiring oral sustained-release morphine. She also began to vomit, the frequency increasing until she was unable to tolerate her oral analgesia. In order to prevent her pain breaking through, the Macmillan nurse suggested that Selina be given morphine suppositories while attempts were made to relieve her vomiting. Selina's pain was successfully controlled in this way. Her vomiting, however, continued to be a problem. The family felt that continued management of pain and vomiting via the rectal route was not ideal. Twenty-four hours later, the Macmillan nurse, in collaboration with both Selina and her family, decided that initiation of a subcutaneous infusion was the most appropriate option.

The child with advanced disease may be unable or unwilling to tolerate oral medication for a variety of reasons, including nausea, vomiting, drowsiness, inability to swallow and/or absence of a gag reflex. If the problem is reversible, a return to managing pain using oral medication may be feasible at a later date.

If a child cannot take oral medication, the rectal route can provide an alternative (see *Figure 5.4*).

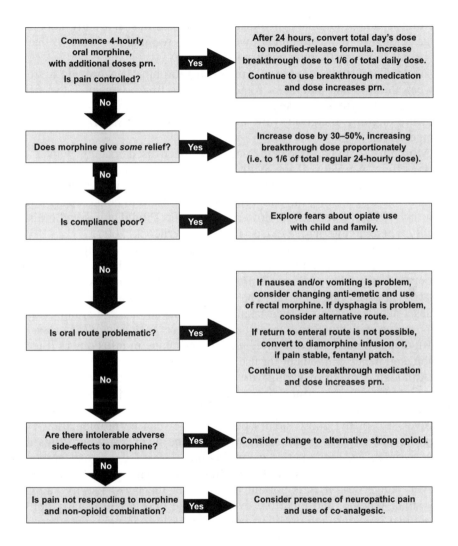

Figure 5.4: Trouble-shooting pain management with strong opioids (K Ballard 03.03)

Morphine suppositories are available in a variety of doses, the smallest being 10 mg. Where smaller doses are required, normal-release morphine suppositories can be divided effectively to obtain the prescribed dose. Dose accuracy, however, cannot be guaranteed. The experience of the WMPMT is that this is not problematic in practice. Suppositories, normally kept in the fridge, should be removed and allowed to reach room temperature so that they can be cut successfully with a sharp knife.

As in *Case study 5.1,* the use of rectal morphine can provide a stopgap between the oral and parenteral routes, allowing time to evaluate the efficacy of changes in symptom management. Rectal morphine can also be utilised to ensure ongoing analgesia while awaiting a community nurse visit to site a syringe driver.

Morphine sustained-release tablets have been used rectally with a slow-release effect. A review of the available literature showed that, although such rectal administration of controlled-release preparations produces variable blood levels of the active drug, the pain relief does not seem to be adversely affected (Gourlay, 1998). Nevertheless, slow-release tablets should only be administered rectally where no alternative exists (Davis and Wilcock, 2001).

If opioids are required by continuous infusion, the subcutaneous or intravenous route can be used. For children who already have a central line or Vascuport in situ, these routes are preferable. For subcutaneous administration, butterfly needles can be used. The WMPMT, however, favours the use of Thalaset needles, owing to their small needle size and ease of siting. Although diamorphine and morphine are equally effective analgesics (Twycross *et al*, 1998), diamorphine is used in preference to morphine in infusions as it is more soluble and hence convenient for use in a syringe driver.

Although a range of syringe drivers is available, the WMPMT routinely uses Graseby MS26 syringe drivers as these are the drivers most familiar to community teams in the West Midlands Region. For breakthrough pain, however, use of the boost facility on this driver can be problematic. A child receiving diamorphine parenterally will often be receiving other drugs in the same syringe, eg. anti-emetics or anxiolytics. Use of the boost facility will obviously give additional quantities of these drugs, which may be unnecessary or even dangerous. It is important to note that the boost facility supplies a very small volume, and therefore even multiple boosts will usually deliver a suboptimal breakthrough dose. To control breakthrough pain, the alternatives shown in *Table 5.2.*should be considered.

Table 5.2: Alternatives for administration of breakthrough medication using a Graseby MS26 syringe driver

⌘ Administration of morphine rectally (equivalent to the amount of opiate received in the infusion in 4 hours*)

⌘ Administration of bolus dose of diamorphine subcutaneously or intravenously (again dosage equivalent to that administered in 4 hours*)

⌘ Administration of oral morphine (equivalent to the amount of opiate received in the infusion in 4 hours*)

⌘ Administration of transmucosal fentanyl (see Section D)

*For dose equivalents of oral and parenteral morphine, and morphine and diamorphine, see Section D

Case study 5.2

Flynn had been requiring regular codeine for pain during his palliative care. It was felt that his pain could be better controlled by oral morphine taken four-hourly. Flynn and his parents were given information about morphine, including the importance of taking it at regular times and the side-effects.

Initially, after commencing the morphine, Flynn became very sleepy. His parents equated this with him being near death and became very anxious until it was reiterated to them that this was a common, but transient side-effect of morphine. His sleepiness subsequently resolved within twenty-four hours.

Thereafter, Flynn was converted to a twice-daily dose of slow-acting morphine and his pain was controlled with no further side-effects. His parents were aware of the breakthrough dose of quick-acting morphine, should it be required, and had commenced a pain diary.

The majority of children can obtain effective pain relief from opioids, as illustrated in *Case study 5.2*. However, continued close assessment is necessary in order to detect early signs of pain breakthrough or side-effects. Side-effects of opioids are well documented and can usually be managed through the interventions described below.

Side-effects of opioids

⌘ **Constipation**: This should be anticipated and laxatives started prophy-lactically. They should be commenced at the same time as the opiate and the importance of regular administration stressed to the family. Laxatives such as codanthramer, which soften the stool as well as increasing the peristaltic action of the bowel, are usually most effective, and mean that the child need only take one laxative preparation. Suppositories or enemas may be required if the problem persists.

⌘ **Nausea and vomiting**: In adults, up to two-thirds of patients receiving morphine experience nausea and vomiting at the outset (Hanks *et al*, 2001). This usually resolves after a few days of administration (Cherny *et al*, 2001). This problem is uncommon in the paediatric palliative population (Beardsmore and Fitzmaurice, 2002). If nausea and/or vomiting is an issue, an anti-emetic is usually effective (Esmail *et al*, 1999). Nevertheless, causes of nausea and vomiting other than opioid administration should always be considered.

⌘ **Sedation**: Sedation is likely, but usually resolves within 24–48 hours of starting the opiate. Somnolence can sometimes recur for a similar period after an increase in dose. Families will benefit from prior warning about this side-effect, as otherwise they may equate a change in conscious level with approaching death.

⌘ **Pruritus**: It has been suggested that pruritus (itching) associated with opioid administration is particularly problematic in teenagers (Zernikowe and Lindena, 2001). The WMPMT's experience, however, indicates that it is most prevalent in babies and can be difficult to control. Good skin care, including treatment of dry skin with an emollient, eg. crotamiton (Eurax) cream, and avoiding soap and overheating may be adequate. Oral rINN (BAN) (chlorpheniramine; Piriton) is often effective (Twycross *et al*, 1998).

⌘ **Respiratory depression**: Although fears of reduced respiratory rate associated with morphine administration are common, research has shown that the presence of pain counteracts the respiratory depressant effect of opiates (Twycross *et al*, 1998). Concern about respiratory depression often leads practitioners to seek monitoring of oxygen saturation. This is unnecessary and potentially a source of additional stress to the family (see *Chapter 2*).

⌘ **Potential addiction**: Carer's fears about addiction to opioids and fears about their side-effects may result in them restricting the amount of medication their child receives (Rhiner *et al*, 1994). In practice, this situation is rarely experienced by the WMPMT, as the importance of highlighting and correcting any likely misconceptions early in the palliative phase is recognised.

Points that may need clarification include:

- initiation of opiates does not imply that the child is very sick or has a short life expectancy

- even during palliation, the use of morphine can be compatible with normal childhood activities, and can be successfully discontinued if pain resolves

- children receiving morphine for pain, even in increasingly high doses, do not crave the drug (Hooke *et al*, 2002).

Nevertheless, children who have received morphine for more than a week will require the dose to be gradually reduced before the drug is stopped (WHO, 1998; Cady, 2001). Failure to do so may result in opiate withdrawal syndrome.

Pain that does not respond to opioids

The number of children who have pain that does not respond to standard analgesia is small. Use of less conventional interventions to control pain before all standard approaches have been exhausted is likely to lead to later questioning of the omitted steps.

Points to consider include:

⌘ Have conventional compounds been used at an appropriate starting dose with appropriate incremental rises if the initial dose was ineffective?
⌘ Has poor compliance compromised the regimen?
⌘ Has malabsorption due to vomiting, diarrhoea or obstruction occurred?
⌘ Is neglected psychological suffering contributing to the child's symptoms?

Neuropathic pain

Neuropathic pain can occur in association with nerve damage or compression, and is often associated with an area of abnormal or absent sensation. In malignant disease, neuropathic pain can be caused by the disease compressing or invading a nerve following surgery, radiotherapy or chemotherapy (peripheral neuropathy), or be due to other causes, such as nerve damage following shingles. Pain described as burning, stinging, stabbing or shooting is likely to be at least partly neuropathic. Symptoms of numbness, or pain on gentle touch, also indicate that the pain originates from a nerve.

Although neuropathic pain may be partially responsive to opiates (Mercadante and Portenoy, 2001) it often requires alternative intervention. If nerve compression is the cause, steroid treatment may be effective in reducing inflammation and thereby lessening pressure on the nerve (Twycross, 1997). The anticonvulsant gabapentin is currently considered to be the best first-line treatment for neuropathic pain (Backonja, 2000; Tremont-Lukats *et al*, 2000), particularly in patients who find touch painful (allodynia) (Backonja, 2000). Some reviews show tricyclic antidepressant drugs, such as amitriptyline, to be equally good (McQuay *et al*, 1996; Watson, 2000). For both drugs the analgesic effect may not be seen for some time: amitriptyline takes three to seven days to take effect, and for gabapentin the dose requires escalation for three to seven days, depending on when a response is seen. Considerable proportions of patients do not obtain good relief with either drug (McQuay *et al*, 1996). Anti-arrhythmic drugs, NSAIDs (Mercadante and Portenoy, 2001), ketamine, calcitonin (Vargas-Schaffer and Pichard-Léandri, 1996) and, as a last resort, spinal analgesia can be tried (Twycross, 1997).

Alternative opioids

If morphine administration results in intolerable side-effects, a change of opioid can be beneficial and should be considered. In one adult study, 80% of patients experienced improvement in their severe side-effects following a switch from morphine to hydromorphone (Lee *et al*, 2001). In adult practice, commonly used alternatives include oxycodone and hydromorphone, both of which are available in immediate-release and sustained-release preparations.

⌘ Hydromorphone may cause less itching, sedation and nausea and vomiting than morphine (Sarhill *et al*, 2001) although mood disturbance may be more likely (Coda *et al*, 1997).

⌘ Oxycodone has been recommended for patients who are troubled by hallucination and sleep disturbance on morphine (Poyhia *et al*, 1993).

The most widely used alternative to morphine in the paediatric setting, however, is fentanyl. The attraction of fentanyl for children is that it can be absorbed through the skin. It is available in a modified-release patch that is changed every three days. Unfortunately, it takes about twelve hours after application of the first dose for the patient to receive a therapeutic quantity of fentanyl, and up to forty-eight hours for a steady blood level to be achieved. When the patch is removed, significant levels persist in the bloodstream for twenty-four hours or more. As a result, fentanyl is unsuitable for patients who have severe uncontrolled pain where it is unclear what the opiate requirement will be. Furthermore, experience indicates that only a minority of children have pain that is sufficiently static to be easily managed with fentanyl patches.

The relatively large dose size of the patches can present difficulties in obtaining the required dose in paediatrics. Division of the patches is not recommended as this may damage their slow-release mechanism.

In adults, fentanyl has been shown to cause less constipation than morphine (Twycross *et al*, 1998) and may also cause less nausea and vomiting (Twycross *et al*, 1998). In c hildren, it is thought to cause less itching than morphine (WHO, 1998). Hunt *et al* (2001) and Collins *et al* (1999) studied the use of fentanyl patches in children receiving palliative care. In the majority of cases, families and professionals found the fentanyl patches to be better than the morphine regimen the child was previously receiving. Side-effects were generally felt to be less. The WMPMT has a variety of experiences of the use of fentanyl patches, including two children in whom a switch from morphine to fentanyl was associated with relief of opioid-related urinary retention.

Recently, transmucosal fentanyl has been produced. This preparation is suitable for the treatment of breakthrough pain. One key advantage is that, because the drug is absorbed through the oral mucous membrane, the patient receives an effective dose more quickly. In a randomised study, adults found that transmucosal fentanyl relieved their breakthrough pain more quickly and more completely than immediate-release morphine (Coluzzi *et al*, 2001). Careful prescribing may be needed as there appears to be no clear relationship between the opioid dose used for background pain and the breakthrough dose (Payne *et al*, 2001). This form of fentanyl is currently only available in a lozenge that should be sucked for fifteen minutes, Some adults have found this to be an unacceptably long period (Burnell-Nugent, 2001) and this is likely to cause problems with cooperation in children.

Methadone can also be a useful alternative opiate. However, great care is needed as dose accumulation may occur (WHO 1998; Guindon *et al*, 2001). Introduction of the drug in the community setting is therefore impractical.

Atypical pain

For most pain, the standard treatments are effective. The following characteristics, however, should alert the practitioner to the need for early consideration of alternative measures:

- intense pain on small movements — pathological fracture
- pain related to breathing — chest infection, pulmonary embolism, fractured rib, or nerve root (Kaye, 1999)
- burning, stabbing pain or unusual sensations (pins and needles) — neuropathic pain
- spasmodic cramping pain in the abdomen — consider bowel colic and bladder spasm.

Non-pharmacological management

It is impossible to separate the physiological and psychological components of pain. Both will impact on how the person perceives, reports, reacts to and copes with his/her pain. The meaning that a child attaches to the pain, eg. 'it hurts because I was naughty' or 'the needle stings but it will make me better', will also in part be determined by his/her social and cultural background.

Measures that enhance wellbeing and/or put the child back in control can modify perception of pain. Those that relax the child or create pleasant stimulation to nerve endings will have physiological effects on the pain via the 'gate' mechanism (Davies and McVicar, 2000b). Specific strategies include:

- distraction (joking, shouting, audio or visual distraction)
- relaxation (rocking/talking to a baby, guiding an older child through muscle relaxation)
- guided imagery (verbalising images of pleasurable situations)
- positive self-talk/thought ('the medicine will take away the pain')
- cutaneous stimulation (rubbing, massage, hot or cold packs, transcutaneous electrical nerve stimulation [TENS])
- hypnosis (requires input of a qualified practitioner).

Eiser (1990) and WHO (1998) explore these techniques further.

It has been reported that children use self-distraction and imagery extensively and successfully (Rhiner *et al*, 1994). Parents also reported the use of various methods of cutaneous stimulation. This considerably eased their feelings of helplessness (Rhiner *et al*, 1994).

Non-pharmacological methods of pain relief can be particularly valuable:

- as an adjunct to pharmacological measures to control pain
- in short-term pain management while analgesic drugs take effect
- in managing other factors, such as tension, that are adding to the pain and rendering analgesics less effective
- in helping to exclude other causes, eg. methods that aid relaxation may elucidate the degree to which anxiety is contributing to the pain.

Pain management with anti-cancer treatment

In some situations, pain relief is best achieved through chemotherapy, radiotherapy or surgery — modalities normally associated with curative intent (see *Chapter 3*). The analgesic effects of such treatments are not immediate. Furthermore, following surgery and radiotherapy, pain may initially be exacerbated. Other measures are therefore vital in the interim.

Section C

Management of symptoms other than pain

In this section, the management of symptoms (excluding pain) will be considered primarily through site-specific disease processes. These will include:

- bone marrow disease
- solid tumours, including thoracic and abdominal disease
- central nervous system (CNS) disease.

To provide a comprehensive and informative section, the West Midlands Paediatric Macmillan Team (WMPMT) has drawn on a wide variety of practical experience to underpin this part of the chapter. This section will encompass the common symptoms seen within these disease processes. It is recognised that pain is commonly associated with paediatric malignant disease progression. The reader is advised to refer to *Section B* of this chapter for the management of pain.

Anxiety potentially pervades many disease processes. It is therefore appropriate to introduce general principles at this point. It will then be considered in more detail, alongside breathlessness, bleeding and nausea.

There are many potential causes of anxiety for the child with cancer. Anxiety and agitation are thought to reflect the child's need to express his/her fears and distress (Goldman, 1998a). A nurse is often well positioned, with the agreement of the family, to explore the causes of the child's fears and provide age-appropriate information. It is important that the child receives continuous reassurance and information regarding his/her symptoms and care. In families where parents do not consent to open communication with the child, this can prove difficult (see *Chapter 4*).

For children who demonstrate anxiety, techniques such as guided imagery and play therapy may aid relaxation and allow an increased sense of control. Complementary therapies such as reflexology or massage may be helpful to some children, but advice should be sought from a trained practitioner, as aromatherapy oils or massage may be contraindicated in some situations. Medication such as diazepam, midazolam and levopromazine are also of benefit for treating anxiety in children during palliative care if other measures fail.

Bone marrow disease

Symptoms of bone marrow failure can be seen in children dying from malignant diseases such as acute lymphoblastic leukaemia, acute myeloid leukaemia and neuroblastoma. The effects of bone marrow failure are due to infiltration of the bone marrow by malignant cells. Pancytopenia occurs as a result of an inability of the bone marrow to produce healthy red, white and platelet cells.

Common signs and symptoms seen in children with bone marrow disease are:

- pallor /lethargy
- bruising/bleeding
- pyrexia.

Lethargy

Lethargy is a common symptom resulting from anaemia. During active treatment, the child's need for blood products is based on regular assessment of full blood counts. A blood transfusion will subsequently be administered once the haemoglobin falls below a predetermined level.

Early in palliation it may be appropriate to check a full blood count if the child shows signs of excessive pallor and tiredness, indicating the possible need for a transfusion. The point at which blood tests and transfusions cease depends upon a number of factors, including: whether transfusions are effective in enhancing the child's quality of life; ease of venous access; and the practicalities of travelling to the hospital to receive transfusions.

Other causes of lethargy that need consideration include low mood and depression, which will require formal assessment and may need pharmacological management. General debilitation due to disease progression and cachexia can also result in the child becoming lethargic.

Bruising/bleeding

As the emphasis of treatment changes to palliation, discussion is needed about the changing criteria for measuring full blood counts and administering blood products. Anxieties about bleeding can evoke vivid, unpleasant images for the child, parents and carers. The majority of children, however, do not have significant bleeding problems, despite a low platelet count (Beardsmore and Alder, 1994). More commonly, severe bruising or petechiae are experienced.

Within the palliative phase of the disease it is considered ideal to treat children wih blood products based upon symptomatology, the intent being to maximise their quality of life with least intervention (Beardsmore and Alder, 1994). For some families, the fear of bleeding will be so great that they will consider the time and energy required to receive a transfusion justified.

Concerns about bleeding can be reduced by helping the family to identify actions that can be taken to minimise the risk, or to deal with bleeding should it occur. Tranexamic acid may be used systemically to prevent bleeding, or topically to control bleeding. The family can be shown how to apply tranexamic acid topically to nostrils or gums during a bleed (see *Case study 5.3*). The use of dark-coloured face cloths and towels during episodes of bleeding can help to mask the distressing visual impact of blood loss.

In cases where a child is distressed by uncontrollable bleeding, the use of parenteral sedation to reduce his/her awareness is appropriate (Regnard and Tempest, 1998). In practice, unless an appropriate infusion is already in place, there is rarely time for this to be set up. If intravenous medication is not available, rectal diazepam may be effective in quickly sedating the child.

Rare causes of bleeding that should be considered include coagulopathy and erosion of major blood vessel by the tumour.

Case study 5.3

Jake was diagnosed with acute lymphoblastic leukaemia at six years of age and had a high white cell count. One year into his treatment he relapsed. A re-induction block of chemotherapy had no impact on his disease. The family opted for no further treatment, but found ongoing visits to the clinic helpful. Having overheard conversations about the risk of bleeding, Jake began to have nightmares about 'all his blood falling out'. His fears were particularly evident during the small nose bleeds that he experienced. Following several sessions with the paediatric community nurse, Jake started to talk about how his teddy had leukaemia and that the bullets would make him bleed. It became clear that Jake had vivid images of violent bleeding from the television. Once his fears had been openly discussed and his misconceptions dispelled, Jake became calmer. He also found it reassuring to have a supply of tranexamic acid at his bedside in case he had a nose bleed at night.

Pyrexia

Pyrexia can present as a result of the disease process or as a symptom of an underlying infection. Where possible, the cause of the pyrexia should be identified; in the case of an infection, the role of antibiotics requires careful consideration and discussion with the family. For more details of the role of antibiotics in palliative care, see *Chapter 1*.

The basic principles of nursing a child with pyrexia should be applied. Excess clothing should be removed and the child should be cared for in a cool well-ventilated room. Tepid sponging may help if the child finds this soothing. Cool drinks can be offered. Paracetamol is the drug of choice for pyrexia. If paracetemol alone is ineffective, the addition of ibuprofen may prove beneficial, although care should be taken in its use with children who have a low platelet count (see *Section A*).

Solid tumours

Children with solid tumours in the palliative phase of their disease may experience symptoms caused by their primary tumour or by metastases. The symptoms commonly encountered will be divided between symptoms occurring in the chest (thoracic disease) and those in the abdomen (abdominal disease).

Thoracic disease

Lung metastases are common in children with solid tumours such as Ewing's sarcoma and osteosarcoma. For others, primary disease in the chest may persist and cause symptoms during the palliative phase.

Common symptoms seen in this group of patients are:

- breathlessness
- cough
- noisy breathing.

Breathlessness

Breathlessness is a distressing symptom, commonly associated with anxiety. Both pharmacological and practical measures can relieve breathlessness. They may be effective in isolation or it may be necessary to use them in combination.

It is important to consider the causes of breathlessness. Respiratory infection can often be relieved by antibiotic therapy. A recognised cause of breathlessness that requires particular consideration is pleural effusion (Ahmedzai, 1995). Drainage of the effusion is an effective way to relieve breathlessness; however, the benefits are usually short-lived, adult studies reporting re-accumulation of the effusion within one month (Anderson *et al*, 1974). Careful consideration should be given to the costs and benefits of drainage. The procedure is invasive and often painful, and the degree of relief obtained is unpredictable, particularly in children whose lung function is affected by concomitant disease processes.

Occasionally, breathlessness can be caused by superior vena caval obstruction. This is considered a palliative emergency and should be suspected in a child who has dilated vessels or soft tissue swelling of the arms, neck or head. High-dose corticosteroids and radiotherapy are often appropriate and effective treatments.

Less common causes, such as pericardial effusion, severe anaemia and heart failure, should also be considered and treated appropriately.

The breathless child should be cared for in a quiet, calm environment. Parents may need help to realise that their anxiety in turn increases their child's anxiety. Cool air from a fan or open window is often effective in improving the child's perception of his/her ability to breathe. Most children also find that adopting an upright, supported position will relieve their breathlessness. An acutely breathless child may benefit from being able to lean forward onto a bed table or similar device.

Where breathlessness is persistent and distressing, drug treatment is indicated. Opioids diminish ventilatory drive, decreasing respiratory effort and the sensation of breathlessness. Opioids may be administered orally or parenterally. Choice of route should be determined by the child's ability to tolerate oral medication. Some authors have suggested the use of nebulised morphine; however, there is little evidence of increased benefit from the use of this route. Indeed, it has been suggested that the absorption of nebulised morphine is unpredictable and therefore best avoided (Expert Working Group of the European Association for Palliative Care, 1996).

Children will sometimes benefit from oxygen therapy, particularly if they have found this helpful in relieving symptoms earlier in treatment. Oxygen therapy in palliation, however, is often misused (Ahmedzai, 1995) and can cause psychological dependence, limit mobility and increase anxiety if given inappropriately (Bredin, 2000). The only measure of the effectiveness of oxygen therapy is the child's perception that it is helpful. In the team's experience, younger children who are unfamiliar with oxygen therapy often see the apparatus necessary for its administration as a further, often frightening, encumbrance. Monitoring of oxygen saturation is unnecessary and likely to cause the child and family additional distress, as the equipment can be seen as an indication of the child's decline.

Anxiety

Anxiety is an almost inevitable consequence of the survival threat brought by breathlessness. Breathlessness is very distressing and can create a great deal of fear and anxiety, in turn exacerbating the symptom (Davis, 1997). Respiratory panic attacks may occur spontaneously, but can also be brought on by exertion (Twycross, 1993) and be associated with acute anxiety. If practical measures, such as positioning and reassurance, prove ineffective, a fast-acting anxiolytic such as sublingual lorazepam is advised (Regnard and Tempest, 1998; Twycross, 1993). The anxiolytic, sedative and muscle-relaxant effects of benzodiazepines (eg. lorazepam and midazolam) can all aid the relief of breathlessness. If all other measures fail, sedation can be considered in order to reduce the child's awareness of his/her breathlessness.

Increasing breathlessness can make it difficult for the child to take oral medication. In some situations, where the child does not have a nasogastric tube in situ, medication will need to be given via a continuous subcutaneous or intravenous infusion.

Case study 5.4

Antony, aged thirteen years, was receiving palliative care for progressive osteosarcoma. Despite surgical excision and further aggressive chemotherapy, his lung metastases continued to progress. Anthony was fully involved in treatment decisions and was aware that his disease was no longer curable. He and his parents decided to commence palliative oral chemotherapy in an attempt to gain some disease control and aid symptom management. After four months of good health, Anthony began to experience coughing episodes that interrupted his sleep at night. Medical review identified no underlying infection and codeine linctus was effectively used as a cough suppressant.

A fortnight later, Anthony developed chest pain and breathlessness on exertion and when lying down. Physical examination and chest X-ray identified a pleural effusion. Anthony was exhausted due to the resultant lack of sleep. Discussions were held with Anthony and his family about the possibility of pleural aspiration. Anthony was reluctant to undergo such a procedure when there was a high possibility of the fluid reaccumulating. MST was commenced to control pain and reduce breathlessness.

Within the month, Anthony became more symptomatic during the day. He experienced breathlessness upon minimal exertion and had episodes, which his parents reported as panic attacks. He was reluctant to discuss issues in great depth and requested medication to help him sleep. Practical measures, such as fan therapy, breathing and relaxation exercises, and finding the optimum position to aid breathing, were discussed. Temazepam was also prescribed with good effect. Humidified oxygen, via an oxygen concentrator, was installed in Anthony's bedroom. Anthony used this, as required, overnight. His parents reported that they believed this was an added security, which helped to allay some of Anthony's anxieties.

In the last few days of Anthony's life, his breathlessness at rest increased significantly. He was no longer able to take oral medication and became more distressed. His symptoms were then controlled by subcutaneous medication administered via a syringe driver. He died peacefully at home eighteen hours after commencing the subcutaneous infusion.

Cough

Cough can be the result of various processes, including pulmonary metastases, heart failure, pleural effusion and chest infection. Identification of the most likely cause is critical to determining the most appropriate treatment. Both cough and chest pain can be the result of bacterial infection in the respiratory tract, and in these cases oral antibiotics are often effective in reducing or eliminating symptoms (Davis, 1997).

A persistent cough can be problematic for the child. A wet cough serves a physiological purpose, and expectoration should therefore not be suppressed. Where the child is unable to expectorate, however, or where the cough is dry, a suppressant is appropriate (Wilcock, 1998), opioids being the best example (Davis, 1997). Codeine, a weak opioid, works by suppressing the cough reflex centre in the brainstem. Morphine is unnecessary unless it is indicated for other reasons, such as uncontrolled pain or dyspnoea (Ahmedzai, 1995), as illustrated in *Case study 5.4*.

Noisy breathing ('death rattle')

Although not a symptom of chest disease, noisy breathing has been included here because of its clear associations.

Children with a significantly reduced level of consciousness will be unable to clear secretions accumulating in their upper airways, resulting in noisy breathing. For some, this noise can be stopped or reduced by a simple change in position. The application of a patch containing hyoscine hydrobromide may also be useful, although it is unlikely to resolve the problem completely as it has no effect on existing secretions, merely reducing further production.

Most families find their child's noisy breathing very difficult to observe. Gentle suction is occasionally beneficial; however, in general it should be avoided in order to prevent stimulation and the production of additional secretions. Families should be reassured that noisy breathing is not an indication of pain or breathing difficulty, and that their child is unaware of the noise.

Abdominal disease

For children with malignancies such as neuroblastoma, abdominal symptoms are often a direct result of their disease. Symptoms commonly seen in children with abdominal disease are: nausea and vomiting; constipation and anorexia.

- nausea and vomiting
- constipation
- anorexia.

Nausea and vomiting

Although often considered as one entity, nausea, vomiting and retching can all occur in isolation as separate symptoms, or in combination. Nausea and vomiting in palliative care can result from one or several concurrent causes. The choice of anti-emetic should be determined by the most likely cause. *Table 5.3* lists the most common causes of vomiting in paediatric palliative care.

The causes listed in *Table 5.3* stimulate the vomiting centre in the brain via a number of pathways (see *Figure 5.5*). In practice, drugs are normally chosen according to the supposed source of emesis. If symptoms are not controlled it is useful to try drugs that have different sites of action. Families who have long-standing experience with anti-emetic therapy during chemotherapy often have faith in one of the $5HT_3$ antagonists, such as ondansetron. These drugs are not ideal, as they have activity in relatively few sites and are expensive; however, studies show that they may have some value in palliative care (Currow *et al*, 1997; Porcel *et al*, 1998). Haloperidol and $5HT_3$ antagonists are useful for the chemical causes of vomiting (Goldman, 1998; Twycross and Back, 1998; Twycross, 1999).

Table 5.3: Common causes of vomiting in paediatric palliative care

Cause	Example
Drugs	Chemotherapy and opiates
Raised intracranial pressure	Due to cerebral tumours or leukaemic infiltration of the central nervous system
Gastric stasis	Hepatomegaly, ascites, constipation, drugs
Biochemical upset	Hypercalcaemia due to disease
Intestinal obstruction	Due to abdominal tumours
Radiotherapy	To the head or abdomen
Anxiety	Concerns regarding medical procedures or the future

Nausea and vomiting are recognised side-effects of opioids (Twycross, 1997), but in the team's experience rarely cause significant problems in children.

In patients with pelvic disease, nausea and vomiting may be caused by gastric stasis. This may result from direct pressure from the tumour, constipation, ascites and hepatomegaly. The underlying cause should be treated where possible. Both metoclopramide and domperidone are useful anti-emetics in the event of gastric stasis (Goldman and Burne, 1998) as they improve passage through the gut.

Abdominal tumours in children rarely result in complete intestinal obstruction.

In the unlikely event of it occurring in paediatric palliative care, abdominal pain and vomiting will be the most common symptoms (Twycross and Wilcock, 2001). Colic, distension, constipation and/or diarrhoea may be present. An abdominal X-ray can help to distinguish between obstruction and faecal impaction (Rawlinson, 2001). In rare cases of children with proven complete obstruction and localised disease, surgical intervention may be an option. For most children, medical management will be the most appropriate strategy. Vomiting cannot always be completely controlled in an obstructed bowel. Medical management consisting of nasogastric tube drainage and anti-emetics may be helpful.

Oral anti-emetic therapy is often difficult in the nauseated child. A rectal preparation such as cyclizine suppositories* can be used to break the vomiting cycle. Once vomiting is controlled, it is often possible to return to using the oral route for the administration of anti-emetics. Should parenteral medication be required, then either cyclizine or levomepromazine can be safely combined with diamorphine in a syringe driver. Levomepromazine is a broad-spectrum anti-emetic and therefore a very useful drug, particularly when the cause of the nausea and/or vomiting is unclear. It is worth noting that levomepromazine has a marked sedative effect, particularly at higher doses. This may be beneficial in the restless and agitated child.

Anxiety can exacerbate nausea, whatever its cause. Reassuring the child therefore, either directly, or indirectly via parental reassurance, of the likely causes of nausea and vomiting and of the treatment plan can be beneficial. The use of relaxation techniques and a calm peaceful environment, particularly at mealtimes, can be useful in reducing anxiety levels and hence nausea.

A proportion of children will require more than one anti-emetic to control their symptoms. However, care must be taken when choosing the combination: for example, antimuscarinics (eg. cyclizine, hyoscine hydrobromide and hyoscine butylbromide) should not be given concurrently with prokinetic drugs (eg. metoclopramide and domperidone) (Twycross *et al*, 1998) because their actions are antagonistic, resulting in loss of effectiveness of both drugs.

Constipation

Constipation can become a significant problem in palliative care, giving rise to abdominal pain, loss of appetite and nausea. Yet it is often eminently preventable through thorough assessment and the application of interventions (Campbell *et al*, 2001). Identification of the likely cause is essential, particularly to exclude intestinal obstruction (see above) as conventional laxative treatments will be damaging in this situation. In children with abdominal disease, constipation may be the result of direct (eg. from tumour) or indirect (eg. from ascites) pressure on the bowel, secondary to immobility, or dehydration from poor fluid intake or vomiting.

---

* These are available as special order medication. They should be ordered in anticipation, as time from order to delivery is at least seven days.

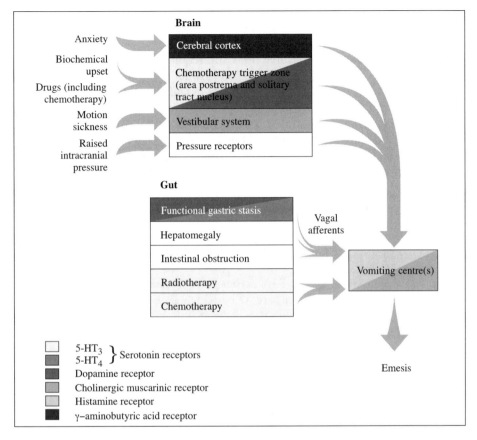

Figure 5.5: Causes of vomiting and mechanism of action of anti-emetics adapted from Goldman (Goldman A [1998] ABC of Palliative Care: special problems of children, anti-emetic flow sheet. *BMJ* **316**: 49–52) **and reproduced by kind permission of the BMJ Publishing Group**

Healthcare professionals should be aware that some drugs, such as opioids, are likely to cause constipation, and should commence a laxative concurrently. Opioids suppress peristalsis in the intestine and increase sphincter tone, which can lead to constipation (Sykes, 1995). Oral laxatives given regularly are ideal in the management of constipation, and are far more acceptable to most children than rectal preparations.

When laxatives are needed, they can be chosen from a range of drugs acting in different ways. Lactulose, which retains fluid in the bowel by osmosis, is often well tolerated by children (Goldman and Burne, 1998). Co-danthramer can be valuable as it combines both a softener and stimulant in one preparation. The sole use of a stimulant laxative, such as senna (Senokot), may cause muscle cramps, and increases the risk of hard stools being passed, which may damage the anal area and cause pain. This in turn exacerbates constipation. In practice, the choice of laxative is often greatly restricted by what the child finds palatable, and unconventional preparations, such as a laxative chocolate, may be the only acceptable solution.

Rectal management of constipation is still required in 25% of patients taking laxatives (Kaye, 1994). Glycerin suppositories act as a lubricant and softener. Suppositories take about 30 minutes to dissolve and therefore defecation within the first five minutes is likely to be due merely to anorectal stimulation. Small-volume enemas, such as Micralax, may be needed if constipation is severe or relief cannot be obtained by other methods.

Professionals should bear in mind that spinal cord compression, dehydration due to pyrexia and biochemical disturbance (eg. hypercalcaemia) can also cause constipation.

Case study 5.5

Ellie, a four-year-old girl receiving palliative care for progressive neuroblastoma, had become increasingly debilitated. Oral opiates were effective in controlling her abdominal pain. Ellie began to vomit if she ate more than a few mouthfuls of food at a time, or if she drank quickly. She consequently became reluctant to take anything orally for fear of vomiting. Full assessment showed that Ellie was constipated, and that due to extensive abdominal disease, gastric stasis was likely to be the cause of her vomiting. Ellie commenced oral co-danthramer with good effect for constipation, and metoclopramide to improve transit through her upper intestinal tract. Ellie's vomiting stopped and she began to eat sweets occasionally, but continued to refuse fluids. Ellie's parents found her poor intake extremely difficult and began to worry that she would dehydrate and that this would cause her death. The likely costs and benefits of artificial feeding and hydration were discussed carefully with Ellie's parents. As Ellie was not complaining of feeling thirsty, they decided that any intervention would bring her more distress than comfort. Ellie's parents concentrated on mouth care and encouraged her to suck small cubes of frozen orange squash.

Anorexia

Loss of appetite (anorexia) is common in children in the palliative phase of their disease. There are many factors that contribute to anorexia, either in isolation or combination. Some, such as nausea, vomiting, sore/dry mouth, pain and constipation, may be partly or fully amenable to treatment.

The ability to feed and nourish a child is fundamental to parenting (Goldman and Burne, 1998). Moreover, it is both rewarding and pleasurable to nurture children, observing them grow stronger and mature. It is common for parents of dying children to equate feeding their child with maintaining hope.

The inability to do so, coupled with observations of weight loss and signs of dehydration in one's child, can be devastating. Western cultures equate anorexia with hastening death (Poole and Froggatt, 2002). Other cultural groups have differing responses, eg. Hindus see anorexia as a sign, rather than a cause, of impending death (Poole and Froggatt, 2002). It is essential that professionals acknowledge the importance that parents attach to nourishing their child and the effects upon them psychologically when they are no longer able to do so.

The question of whether palliative patients should be artificially supported with food and/or fluids is controversial and has prompted debate within adult palliative care (Holmes, 1998; Jans Meares, 2000). This debate is largely concerned with whether to feed or simply hydrate patients, the range of expectations of individual families, and the needs of healthcare professionals to be seen to be 'doing something'.

The place where the child is being cared for can influence the decision as to whether a child receives artificial hydration. Clearly, within a hospital setting the delivery of intravenous fluids is achievable; whether it is the best option, however, remains questionable. This decision will be influenced by several factors, including:

- adequate venous access
- the child's and family's views on the siting of a cannula
- the presence of symptoms that might be relieved by hydration.

In practice, there is a risk that in an acute inpatient setting the administration of intravenous fluids will take place as a matter of routine. For some children, the decision to change from active treatment to palliation may happen while they are inpatients, in which case an intravenous infusion may already be in situ. For the child and family to be empowered in the palliative phase of the disease, healthcare professionals will need to discuss the pros and cons of an infusion. If the child is complaining of thirst and is unable to swallow, the insertion of a cannula for fluids is likely to be acceptable and offer relief. If the cannula is merely to provide venous access, healthcare professionals should consider removing it.

Most children receiving palliative care for a malignancy will be nursed at home. In this setting, the administration of intravenous fluids is impractical even if a child has central venous access. In practice, the community team have limited capacity to constantly staff the child's home. It is therefore difficult to provide safe care of a child receiving intravenous fluids. Although hypodermoclysis (infusion of fluids subcutaneously) has been used in adult palliation, this has not generally been transposed to the paediatric setting.

Healthcare professionals can provide practical advice to families about dietary intake, such as offering small amounts of nicely presented, favourite foods and including the sick child at family mealtimes, even if he/she is reluctant to eat. Food supplements can be a helpful addition, but should be introduced with the input of a paediatric dietitian. Sick children are nevertheless likely to continue to have poor nutritional intake, which may worsen as their condition deteriorates.

It is the team's practice to guide families away from invasive interventions such as nasogastric feeding. The introduction of enteral feeding for children in the palliative phase of their disease needs careful consideration, taking into account the potential benefits and burdens (Scanlon, 1998). The siting of a nasogastric tube is an unpleasant, undignified and invasive procedure at any time, particularly in the palliative phase, when comfort and dignity are the objectives. The use of nasogastric feeding can, however, prove to be the most acceptable option when the alternative is thirst and hunger. The paediatric dietitian will provide guidance on the frequency and type of feed, considering the unique needs of each child and family.

In the team's experience, many families find it valuable to be given the flexibility to adjust their child's nasogastric feeds as they see appropriate, returning their control in an area of basic parenting. It is more difficult to discontinue than to commence feeds (Holmes, 1998) and particularly difficult to discontinue feeds that were instituted prior to palliative care. In such circumstances, families may consider the withdrawal of nutritional support synonymous with hastening death (Holmes, 1998), and in religions such as the Jewish faith this is not acceptable (Schostak, 1994). With explanation, most families understand the change in emphasis during palliation, and begin to see food and drink as valuable when they are a source of pleasure to the child (see *Case study 5.5*).

Central nervous system disease (CNS)

Symptoms of CNS disease are seen in primary and secondary disease processes. In paediatric palliative care, the diseases in which they are likely to occur include brain tumours and leukaemia. Common symptoms in patients with CNS disease are:

- nausea and vomiting
- seizures
- communication difficulties.

Patients with primary CNS disease, eg. brain tumours, will be expected to experience such symptoms. Other patients, such as those with leukaemia, may develop secondary CNS disease at relapse or during the palliative phase of their disease.

Nausea and vomiting

Nausea and vomiting frequently occur when CNS involvement is present. In the child known to have CNS disease, anti-emetics should be prescribed in readiness for this potential problem. Cyclizine is the drug of choice for centrally driven nausea and vomiting, and also has the advantage of being available as suppositories for rectal administration. Timing can be crucial in the administration of anti-emetics, with cyclizine requiring eight-hourly administration for optimum effectiveness.

Ondansetron or hyoscine hydrobromide patch (Scopoderm) can provide useful adjuncts if cyclizine alone does not control nausea and vomiting. The WMPMT have found Scopoderm particularly useful in children with brainstem disease – infrequently in isolation, usually in conjunction with cyclizine. Should control remain a problem, a continuous infusion of medications may be required. Cyclizine can be used in continuous infusion and is compatible with a range of other drugs commonly used in palliative care (Kaye, 1994).

Seizures

Seizures are commonly seen in CNS disease and should be anticipated. Management should therefore be discussed with the family and a clear strategy put in place, including advice on positioning and the relevant medication available. Seizure activity can range from short absences to grand-mal events. This discussion will primarily focus on the management of grand-mal seizures.

Rectal diazepam is useful in controlling both generalised and local seizures. It works within ten to fifteen minutes, with the effect lasting for about three hours (Obbens, 1994). A stock of rectal diazepam should be prescribed and dispensed to the family and be stored at the home in a place that is easily and quickly accessible. Many parents, with support and guidance, will administer rectal diazepam if necessary. Should they be reluctant, community staff should be alerted and, where possible, be prepared to visit and administer the drug. The child may, however, recover without medication.

The *Paediatric Advanced Life Support – Resuscitation Guidelines* (Resuscitation Council (UK) 2000) recommend intravenous lorazepam as a first-line treatment of seizures; however, the WMPMT do not routinely use lorazepam in palliative care. Buccal midazolam has been found to be as effective as rectal diazepam in the acute treatment of seizures, with administration being more socially acceptable and convenient (Scott *et al*, 1999). For uncontrolled seizures, paraldehyde, administered rectally, can be effective but is rarely required.

Should a child have had seizures previously or be on prophylactic anticonvulsant medication, it is important that the regular therapy is reviewed following new seizure activity. A child who has previously not required anticonvulsants is likely to be commenced on one following a seizure. As disease progresses, however, seizures can become difficult to control, even with manipulation of oral anticonvulsant therapy.

As disease progresses, many children will require a continuous infusion of medication. Midazolam is considered the drug of choice for continuous infusion. It is also compatible with diamorphine, cyclizine, haloperidol and hyoscine — drugs commonly used in the palliative phase of disease (Kaye, 1994).

Other potential causes of seizures in paediatric palliative care include cerebral metastases, electrolyte imbalance and fever.

Communication difficulties

Patients with brainstem disease can develop slurred or nasal speech because of poor movement of the tongue, lips and palate. In those with disease of the dominant hemisphere, difficulty with understanding the spoken and written word and/or speaking and writing may be a problem (Clarke, 1995). As disease advances, these symptoms may occur and are also likely to progress. This may result in serious communication difficulty.

Speech and language therapists are crucial in determining the degree of the problem and the most suitable tools to meet the individual needs of the child. Assessment can be carried out at home and therapists will offer suggestions and instruct the family in use of the tools. Children who may benefit from electronic communication aids will be referred to regional 'Access to communication technology centres'. The use of such aids, however, requires some skill and dexterity, which younger children may not possess.

Swallowing difficulties

Progressive disease in the CNS can affect the ability to swallow. Like slurred speech, this is particularly seen in children with brainstem tumours, with both symptoms frequently occurring simultaneously. Impaired swallowing has been described as one of the most distressing symptoms (Collins *et al*, 2002). Children may be otherwise reasonably well, but their swallowing will be compromised. Observation for early signs of difficulty and prompt action will minimise the risk of problems such as aspiration. Parents should be encouraged to observe the child for signs of difficulty (eg. coughing or choking with food or fluid). Assessment by a speech and language therapist is advisable when problems become apparent. At the onset of symptoms, food may be well tolerated but fluids may cause problems. The provision of thickened liquids may be all that is required at this point. Further progression, however, frequently results in it becoming unsafe for the child to continue to receive food or fluids by mouth, and it is therefore usually necessary to pursue alternative ways of providing feeding (nasogastric feeding), as illustrated in *Case study 5.6*.

Children who still wish to experience the pleasure of tasting food may wish to chew and then spit food out. When a child is taking nothing by mouth, regular mouth care is advised to maintain cleanliness and comfort.

Case study 5.6

Tom, aged ten years, had a brainstem tumour and was in the palliative phase of his disease. He was generally well, but had increasingly slurred speech and had begun to have choking episodes when drinking. Thickened fluids helped for a short time but the choking episodes became more frequent. An assessment by the speech and language therapist confirmed that it was no longer safe for him to take oral fluids. The risk of aspiration was explained to Tom and his parents and it was advised that he should receive nasogastric feeds. They agreed to have a nasogastric tube passed and Tom's mum was taught how to administer bolus feeds, which they gave during waking hours. Feed type, regularity and volume were established following discussion with the dietitian.

Tom lived for a further two months. Although he required medication for vomiting, he continued to receive nasogastric feeds, the timing and volume of which his family altered, depending on his ability to tolerate them. Regular mouth care was also undertaken.

Summary

Providing symptom control for a child receiving palliative care requires the input of specialist practitioners. Many factors that will need to be taken into consideration require a multidisciplinary approach to its provision. Thorough and repeated assessment is the mainstay of good symptom control management. A systematic and evidence-based response from all members of the multidisciplinary team can ensure optimum symptom relief for the child. Experienced practitioners will describe how no two children are the same and each palliative episode is unique. There is, however, a wealth of knowledge available from personal narratives and the literature, which can guide even the most junior staff. The content and format presented here should add to that body of knowledge.

References

Ahmedzai S (1995) Palliation of respiratory symptoms. In: Doyle D, Hanks G, MacDonald N (Eds). *Oxford Textbook Of Palliative Medicine*. Oxford University Press, Oxford: 349–76

Anderson CB, Philpot GW, Ferguson TB (1974) The treatment of malignant effusion. *Cancer* **33**: 916–22

Association for Children with Life-threatening or Terminal Conditions and their Families (ACT) and the Royal College of Paediatrics and Child Health (RCPCH) (1997) *A Guide to the Development of Children's Palliative Care Services*. ACT/ RCPCH, London

Backonja MM (2000) Anticonvulsants (antineuropathics) for neuropathic pain syndromes. *Clin J Pain* **16**(2, Suppl): S67–72

Beardsmore S, Alder S (1994) Terminal care at home – the practical issues. In: Hill L (Ed). *Caring for Dying Children and Their Families*. Chapman and Hall, London: 162–76

Beardsmore S, Fitzmaurice N (2002) Palliative care in paediatric oncology. *Eur J Cancer* **38**(14): 1900–7

Benner P (1984) *From Novice to Expert: Excellence and Power in Clinical Nursing Practice*. Addison-Wesley, California

Bloom BJ (2001) New drug therapies for pediatric rheumatic diseases. *Curr Opin Rheumatol* **13**(5): 410–14

Bredin M (2000) The management of breathlessness in advanced cancer. *Oncology Nurses Today* **5**(1): 20–3

British National Formulary (BNF) 47 March 2004. British Medical Association and Royal Pharmaceutical Society of Great Britain, London

Brookes G (2000) Children's competency to consent – a framework for practice. *Paediatr Nurs* **12** (5): 31–35

Burnell-Nugent M (2001) Oral transmucosal fentanyl citrate in the clinical setting. *Eur J Palliat Care* **8**(6, Suppl): 9–11

Cady J (2001) Understanding opioid tolerance in cancer pain. *Oncol Nurs Forum* **28**(10): 1561–8

Campbell T, Draper S, Reid J, Robinson L (2001) The management of constipation in people with advanced cancer. *Int J Palliat Nurs* **7**(3): 110–19

Carter B (1994) *Child and Infant Pain: Principles of nursing care and management*. Chapman and Hall, London: 42–63

Cherny N, Ripamonti C, Pereira J *et al* (2001) Strategies to manage the adverse effects of oral morphine: an evidence-based report. *J Clin Oncol* **19**(9): 2542–54

Clarke SD (1995) Speech therapy. In: Doyle D, Hanks G, MacDonald N (Eds). *Oxford Textbook of Palliative Medicine*. Oxford University Press, Oxford: 551

Coda BA, O'Sullivan B, Donaldson G *et al* (1997) Comparative efficacy of patient-controlled administration of morphine, hydromorphone, or sufentanil for the treatment of oral mucositis pain following bone marrow transplantation. *Pain* **72**(3): 333–46

Collins JJ, Dunkel IR, Gupta SK *et al* (1999) Transdermal fentanyl in children with cancer pain: feasibility, tolerability, and pharmacokinetic correlates. *J Pediatr* **134**(3): 319–23

Collins JJ, Devine TD, Dick GS *et al* (2002) The measurement of symptoms in young children with cancer: the validation of the Memorial Symptom Assessment Scale in children aged 7-12. *J Pain Symptom Manage* **23**(1): 10–16

Coluzzi PH, Schwartzberg L, Conroy JD *et al* (2001) Breakthrough cancer pain: a randomised trial comparing oral transmucosal fentanyl citrate (OTFC®) and morphine sulfate immediate release (MSIR®). *Pain* **91**: 123–30

Cooley C, Adeodu S, Aldred H *et al* (2000) Paediatric palliative care: a lack of research-based evidence. *Int J Palliat Nurs* **6**(7): 346–51

Currow DC, Coughlan M, Fardell B, (1997) Use of ondansetron in palliative medicine. *J Pain Symptom Manage* **13**: 302–7

Davies J, McVicar A (2000a) Issues in effective pain control. 1: Assessment and education. *Int J Palliat Nurs* **6**(2): 58–65

Davies J, McVicar A (2000b) Issues in effective pain control. 2: From assessment to management. *Int J Palliat Nurs* **6**(4): 162–9

Davis C (1997) ABC of palliative care: breathlessness, cough and other respiratory problems. *BMJ* **315**: 931–4

Davis C (2000) A new 24-hour morphine hydrogel suppository. *Euro J Palliat Care* **7**(5): 165–7

Davis M, Wilcock A (2001) Modified-release opioids. *Eur J Palliat Care* **8**(4): 142–6

Eiser C (1990) *Chronic Childhood Disease: An introduction to psychology theory and research.* Cambridge University Press, Cambridge

Eland JM (1988) Persistence of pain research: one nurse researcher's efforts. *Recent Adv Nurs* **21**: 43–61

Esmail Z, Montgomery C, Courtrn C, Kestle J (1999) Efficacy and complications of morphine infusions in postoperative paediatric patients. *Paediatr Anaesth* **9**(4): 321–7

Expert Working Group of the European Association for Palliative Care (1996) Morphine in cancer pain: modes of administration. *BMJ* **312**: 823–6

Farrington A (1993) Intuition and expert clinical practice in nursing. Education and debate. *Br J Nurs* **2**(4): 228–33

Ferrell BR, Rhiner M, Shapiro B, Dierkes M (1994) The experience of pediatric cancer pain. Part I: Impact of pain on the family. *J Pediatr Nurs* **9**(6): 368–79

Fitzmaurice N, McKeag G, Bradwell M, Hyne J (1997) Equipment cases for palliative care. *Paediatr Nurs* **9**(6): 18–19

Goldman A (1998a) ABC of palliative care: special problems of children. *Br Med J* **316**: 49–52

Goldman A (1998b) Palliative care for children. In: Faull C, Carter Y, Woof R (Eds). *The Handbook of Palliative Care.* Blackwell Scientific, London: 256–71

Goldman A (2001) Recent advances in palliative care. *BMJ* **322**: 234

Goldman A, Burne R (1998) Symptom management. In: Goldman A (Ed). *Care of the Dying Child.* Oxford University Press, Oxford: 52–75

Gourlay GK (1998) Sustained relief of chronic pain: pharmacokinetics of sustained release morphine. *Clinical Pharmacokinetics* **35**(3): 173–90

Guindon C, Averous V, Jami H, Albanesi E (2001) Terminal cancer pain. *Eur J Palliat Care* **8**(2): 49–53

Hanks GW, Conno F, Cherny N *et al* (2001) Morphine and alternative opioids in cancer pain: the EAPC recommendations. *Br J Cancer* **84**(5): 587–93

Hilden JM, Emanuel EJ, Fairclough DL *et al* (2001) Attitudes and practices among paediatric oncologists regarding end-of-life care: results of the 1998 American Society of Clinical Oncology survey. *J Clin Oncol* **19**(1): 205–12

Holmes S (1998) The challenge of providing nutritional support to the dying. *Int J Palliat Nurs* **4**(7): 26–31

Hooke C, Brown Hellsten M, Stutzer C, Forte K (2002) Pain management for the child with cancer in end-of-life care: APON position paper. *J Pediatr Oncol Nurs* **19**(2): 43–7

Hunt A, Goldman A, Devine T, Phillips M (2001) Transdermal fentanyl for pain relief in a paediatric palliative care population. *Palliat Med* **15**(5): 405–12

Jans Meares C (2000) Nutritional issues in palliative care. *Semin Oncol Nurs* **16**(2): 135–45

Jeffrey D (1993) Informed consent. In: *'There Is Nothing More I Can Do!' An introduction to the ethics of palliative care*. Patten Press, Cornwall

Kart T, Christrup LL, Rasmussen M (1997) Recommended use of morphine in neonates, infants and children based on a literature review. Part 1: Pharmacokinetics. *Paediatr Anaesth* **7**: 5–11

Kaye P (1994) *A–Z Pocketbook of Symptom Control*. EPL Publications, Northampton

Kaye P (1999) *Decision Making in Palliative Care*. EPL Publications, Northampton

Lee MA, Leng ME, Tiernan EJ (2001) Retrospective study of the use of hydromorphone in palliative care patients with normal and abnormal urea and creatinine. *Palliat Med* **15**(1): 26–34

Lenz ER, Pugh LC, Milligan RA, Gift A, Suppe F (1997) The middle-range theory of unpleasant symptoms. *ANS Adv Nurs Sci* **19**(3): 14–27

Macdonald S (2002) Aspirin use to be banned in under 16 year olds. *Br Med J* **325**: 988

McQuay HJ, Tramer M, Nye BA *et al* (1996) A systematic review of antidepressants in neuropathic pain. *Pain* **68**(2-3): 217–27

Mercadante S, Portenoy RK (2001) Opioid poorly-responsive cancer pain. Part 3: Clinical Strategies to improve opioid responsiveness. *J Pain Symptom Manage* **21**(4): 338–54

Obbens EAMT (1994) Neurological problems in palliative medicine. In: Doyle D, Hanks G, MacDonald N (1995) *Oxford Textbook of Palliative Medicine*. Oxford University Press, Oxford: 460–72

Payne R, Coluzzi P, Hart L *et al* (2001) Long-term safety of oral transmucosal fentanyl citrate for breakthrough cancer pain. *J Pain Symptom Manage* **22**: 575–83

Poole K, Froggatt K (2002) Loss of weight and loss of appetite in advanced cancer: a problem for the patient, the carer or the health professional? *Palliat Med* **16** (6): 499–506

Porcel JM, Salud A, Porta J *et al* (1998) Antiemetic efficacy of subcutaneous 5-HT$_3$ receptor antagonists in terminal cancer patients. *J Pain Symptom Manage* **15**: 265–6

Poyhia R, Vaimo A, Kalso E, (1993) A review of oxycodone's clinical pharmacokinetics and pharmacodynamics. *J Pain Symptom Manage* **8**: 63–7

Pursell E (1994) Physical symptom control in children who are dying. *J Cancer Care* **3**: 315

Quill TE, Billings JA (1998) Palliative care textbooks come of age. *Ann Intern Med* **129**: 590–4

Rawlinson F (2001) Malignant bowel obstruction. *Eur J Palliat Care* **8**(4): 137–40

Regnard CFB, Tempest S (1998) *A Guide to Symptom Relief in Advanced Cancer*. 4th edn. Hochland and Hochland Ltd, Hale, Cheshire

Resuscitation Council (UK) (2000) *Paediatric Advanced Life Support – Resuscitation Guidelines*. Resuscitation Council UK, London

Rhiner M, Ferrell BR, Shapiro B, Dierkes M (1994) The Experience of Pediatric Cancer Pain. Part II: Management of Pain. *J Pediatr Nurs* **9**(6): 380–7

Ross DM, Ross SA (1984) The importance of type of question, psychological climate and subject set in interviewing children about pain. *Pain* **19**(1): 71–9

Sarhill N, Walsh D, Nelson KA (2001) Hydromorphone: pharmacology and clinical applications in cancer patients. *Support Care Cancer* **9**(2): 84–96

Scanlon C (1998) Unravelling ethical issues in palliative care. *Semin Oncol Nurs* **14**(2): 137–44

Schostak RZ (1994) Jewish ethical guidelines for resuscitation and artificial nutrition and hydration of the dying elderly. *J Med Ethics* **20**: 93–100

Scott R, Beasag F, Neville B (1999) Buccal midazolam and rectal diazepam for treatment of prolonged seizures in childhood and adolescence: a randomised trial. *Lancet* **353**: 623–6

Sykes NP (1995) Constipation and diarrhoea. In: Doyle D, Hanks G, MacDonald N (Eds). *Oxford Textbook of Palliative Medicine*. Oxford University Press, Oxford: 299–310

Tobias JD (2000) Weak analgesica and nonsteroidal anti-inflammatory agents in the management of children with acute pain. *Pediatr Clin North Am* **47**(3): 527–43

Tremont-Lukats IW, Megeff C, Backonja MM (2000) Anticonvulsants for neuropathic pain syndromes: mechanisms of action and place in therapy. *Drugs* **60**(5): 1029–52

Twycross R (1993) Symptom control: the problem areas. *Palliat Med* **7**(Suppl 1): 1–8

Twycross R (1997) *Symptom Management in Advanced Cancer*. 2nd edn. Radcliffe Medical Press, Abingdon

Twycross R (1999) Guidelines for the management of nausea and vomiting. *Palliative Care Today* **7** (4): 32–4

Twycross R, Back I (1998) Nausea and vomiting in advanced cancer. *Eur J Palliat Care* **5**(2): 39–45

Twycross R, Wilcock A (2001) *Symptom Management in Advanced Cancer*. 3rd edn. Radcliffe Medical Press, Abingdon

Twycross R, Wilcock A, Thorp S (1998) *Palliative Care Formulary*. Radcliffe Medical Press, Abingdon

Vargas-Schaffer G, Pichard-Léandri E (1996) Neuropathic pain in young children with cancer. *Eur J Palliat Care* **3**(3): 95–8

Watson CP (2000) The treatment of neuropathic pain: antidepressants and opioids. *Clin J Pain* **16**(2, Suppl): S49–55

Wilcock A (1998) The Management of Respiratory Symptoms. In: Faull C, Carter Y, Woof R (Eds). *The Handbook of Palliative Care*. Blackwell Scientific, London: 157–76

Wolfe W, Grier HE, Klar N *et al* (2000) Symptoms and suffering at the end of life in children with cancer. *N Engl J Med* **342**: 326–33

Wong DL, Baker CM (1988) Pain in children: comparison of assessment scales. *Pediatr Nurs* **14**: 9–17

World Health Organization (1998) *Cancer Pain Relief and Palliative Care in Children*. WHO, Geneva

Zernikowe B, Lindena G (2001) Long-acting morphine for pain control in paediatric oncology. *Med Pediatr Oncol* **36**(4): 451–8

Section D

Symptom control guidelines

Symptom Control and Palliative Care in Children with Cancer

Recommended drug doses

Departments of Haematology, Oncology and Pharmacy
The Birmingham Children's Hospital NHS Trust

Revised April 2003

Prepared by
Mr N Ballantine, Specialist Clinical Pharmacist

DRUGS, DOSES, ROUTES OF ADMINISTRATION AND SIDE-EFFECTS

Average weights: At 1 year =10kg; at 2 years = 12kg; at 4 years = 16kg; at 10 years = 35kg

NB. Suggested dose is an individual dose unless otherwise stated

DRUG / Indication	Route	Times per day	DOSE 0–4 weeks	4 weeks to 2 years	2–12 years	12 years and over	Availability	Comments	Dose ref
AMITRIPTYLINE									
Co-analgesia	Oral	1 at night			0.5–2mg/kg	30–150mg	Tablet: 10mg, 25mg, 50mg. Mixture (SF): 10mg in 5ml	Dangerous in overdose. Increase dose to achieve effect. For nerve infiltration pain, opiates are not indicated	4
Depression	Oral	1 at night		1–2mg/kg					4
CARBAMAZEPINE									
Co-analgesic	Oral	2		Initially 5mg/kg/day in two divided doses, increasing by 2.5mg/kg/day at weekly intervals to 10–20mg/kg/day		100–200mg/day increasing to 800–1200mg/day	Tablet: 100mg, 200mg, 400mg. Chewable tablet: 100mg, 200mg. Modified-release tablet: 200mg, 400mg. Liquid (SF): 100mg in 5ml	Increase every 3–7 days to achieve effect. For nerve infiltration pain, opiates are not indicated. Plasma level monitoring desirable – therapeutic range 4–14mg/l. Modified-release tablets may be divided across the score mark, but must NOT be crushed or chewed	3
CHLORPHENAMINE (CHLORPHENIRAMINE) Antihistamine	Oral	2			1mg		Tablet: 4mg. Syrup: 2mg in 5ml	Oral dose may safely be doubled	3

Chlorphenamine age ranges: <1 year | 2–5 years | 6–12 years | ≥12 years

Route	Times per day	<1 year	2–5 years	6–12 years	≥12 years	Availability	Dose ref
Oral	3		1–2mg	2–4mg	4mg		3
SC/IV	Single	0.25mg/ml	>1 year: 2.5–5mg	10mg		Injection:	3

DRUG	Indication	Route	Times per day	0–4 weeks	4 weeks to 2 years	2–12 years	12 years and over	Availability	Comments	Dose ref
CO-DANTHRAMER	Laxative	Oral	1	2.5–5ml of 25/200mg in 5ml				Suspension: 25/200mg in 5ml, 75/1000mg in 5ml. Capsule: 25/200mg, 37.5/500mg	Co-danthramer is a mixture of dantron and poloxomer 188 in the proportions stated	2
CODEINE PHOSPHATE	Antitussive, antidiarrhoeal	Oral	4–6	0.5mg/kg			15–30mg	Tablet: 15mg, 30mg, 60mg. Syrup: 15mg in 5ml	Doses >60mg unlikely to offer additional benefit. Use stronger opiate	4
	Analgesic	Oral	4–6	0.5–1mg/kg			30–60mg			4
CROTAMITON (Eurax®)	Anti-pruitic	Topical	1	<3 years — Apply to affected area(s)		>3 years — Apply to affected area(s)		Cream: 30g and 100g. Lotion: 100ml		1
			2–3							1
CYCLIZINE	Anti-emetic	Oral / Rectal	3		1mg/kg	12.5–25mg	25–50mg	Tablet: 50mg. Suppositories: 12.5mg, 25mg, 50mg. Special	Compatible with diamorphine in ratio of 1:1 up to 20mg/ml. Increase in concentration of one component above 20mg/ml requires reduction in the other	4
		SC/IV	Continuous	Total daily dose as for oral				Injection: 50mg in 1 ml		4

DOSE — N.B. Suggested dose is an individual dose unless otherwise stated

DRUG / Indication	Route	Times per day	DOSE N.B. Suggested dose is an individual dose unless otherwise stated				Availability	Comments	Dose ref
			0–4 weeks	4 weeks to 2 years	2–12 years	12 years and over			
DEXAMETHASONE Cerebral pressure symptoms, cord compression and acute tissue swelling	Oral	2–3	Initially 100µg/kg, then 50µg/kg every 6 hours, changing to oral for maintenance				Tablet: 0.5mg, 2mg. Liquid (SP): 2mg in 5ml	Use short course and taper quickly	1
Supplementary anti-emetic	IV	Single dose	≤15kg: 1mg 16–25kg: 2mg 26–35kg: 3mg 36–45kg: 4mg 46–55kg: 5mg >55kg: 6mg				Injection: 4mg in 1ml		
DIAMORPHINE Analgesic	Oral	4-hourly	<6 months 100µg/kg		>6 months 200µg/kg OR 1/6 of TOTAL daily dose of sustained-release morphine		Tablet: 10mg	Dosage should always be adjusted to the needs of the patient – starting doses are given. Dose increments should be 30–50%, according to the patient's condition. No therapeutic advantage over morphine by oral route, but tablets are soluble	3, 4

DRUG Indication	Route	Times per day	DOSE — N.B. Suggested dose is an individual dose unless otherwise stated				Availability	Comments	Dose ref
			0–4 weeks	4 weeks to 2 years	2–12 years	12 years and over			
DIAMORPHINE Analgesic	SC infusion	Continuous	15µg/kg/hour		20µg/kg/hour OR 1/3 of the total daily oral dose of sustained-release morphine		Injection: 5mg, 10mg, 30mg, 100mg, 500mg	Solubility is 1g in 1.6ml at 25°C, giving 2.4ml of solution. Use Water for Injection to reconstitute if concentration required >50mg/ml. Add 25mg hydrocortisone to each syringe if SC sites become inflamed, or use hyaluronidase. Compatible in syringe with cyclizine, haloperidol, hyoscine and methotrimeprazine – see notes on these drugs for further information	4
Dyspnoea	Nebuliser	3–4 hourly	2.5mg in 2ml Sodium Chloride 0.9%						1
DIAZEPAM Sedation	Oral	2–3			2–3mg	2–10mg	Tablet: 2mg, 5mg, 10mg. Suspension: 2mg in 5ml	Caution: Transient respiratory depression possible by all routes. Antidote: flumazenil (Anexate)	3
Muscle spasm	Oral	2–4	250µg/ml	0.5–3mg		1.5–15mg			3
Continuing convulsions	IV	Continuous	50µg/kg/hour (Maximum: 300µg/kg/hour)	100µg/kg/hour (Maximum: 400µg/kg/hour)		125µg/kg/hour	Injection: 10mg in 1ml	Titrate dose according to response. Use Diazemuls for continuous infusion. IV only – too irritant SC	3

DOSE
N.B. Suggested dose is an individual dose unless otherwise stated

DRUG / Indication	Route	Times per day	0–4 weeks	4 weeks to 2 years	2–12 years	12 years and over	Availability	Comments	Dose ref
DIAZEPAM Continuing convulsions	Rectal	Single dose	1.25–2.5mg	5mg	5–10mg	10mg	Rectal solution in single dose tube: 2.5mg, 5mg, 10mg	Use Valium injection rectally for doses <2.5mg. Otherwise use Stesolid. Dose may be repeated ONCE only after 5 minutes. If no effect after two doses, consider midazolam	3
DICLOFENAC Analgesic	Oral Rectal	3			0.3–1mg/kg		Tablet: 25mg 50mg. Dispersible tablet: 50mg. Suppository: 12.5mg, 100mg		3
	Oral sustained release	1			2–3mg/kg		Sustained-release tablet: 75mg, 100mg		1

			>1 year	>4 years	12 years and over			
DIHYDROCODEINE Analgesia	Oral	4–6 hourly	500µg/kg	0.5–1mg/kg	30mg	Tablet: 30mg. Syrup: 10mg in 5ml	Likely to cause severe constipation. Have a low threshold for change to strong opiate	3

DRUG / Indication	Route	Times per day	DOSE — N.B. Suggested dose is an individual dose unless otherwise stated				Availability	Comments	Dose ref
			0–4 weeks	4 weeks to 2 years	2–12 years	12 years and over			
FENTANYL Opioid analgesic	Topical	Every 3 days			Please refer to Appendix I for further information on transferring patients to fentanyl patches		Self-adhesive patch: 2.5mg 5mg 7.5mg 10mg	provides 25µg per hour provides 50µg per hour provides 75µg per hour provides 100µg per hour **Caution:** The full effect is not achieved until 24–48 hours after the first patch is applied. Use oral morphine sulphate for breakthrough pain. On withdrawing treatment, serum fentanyl levels insignificant only after a further 3 days	1
GABAPENTIN Neuropathic pain	Oral	3			10–13mg/kg	300–800mg	Capsule: 100mg, 300mg, 400mg	Commence with lowest dose daily on day 1, increase to twice daily on day 5, and thrice daily on day 10. Further adjust dose according to response. Doses given are target maintenance doses. Adjust dose in renal failure	3

DRUG	Indication	Route	Times per day	DOSE N.B. Suggested dose is an individual dose unless otherwise stated				Availability	Comments	Dose ref
				0–4 weeks	4 weeks to 2 years	2–12 years	12 years and over			
HALOPERIDOL	Sedation and anti-emetic	Oral	2			25µg/kg (Max: 5mg)	0.5–2mg	Tablet: 1.5mg, 5mg, 10mg, 20mg. Capsule: 0.5mg. Liquid: (SF): 5mg in 5ml, 10mg in 5ml, 50mg in 5ml	Consider a change to levomepromazine if dose required >10mg per day	3, 4
		SC/IV	Continuous			25–50µg/kg/day		Injection: 5mg in 1ml	Compatible with diamorphine (10–100mg/ml) at concentrations between 2–4mg/ml in syringe. Physically compatible with morphine in syringe ± other drugs	4
HEPARIN	Line flushing	IV	As required		≤1 year: 5 units in 5ml	>1 year Hickman: 25 units in 2.5ml Vascuport: 500 units in 5ml		Injection: (SP) 1 unit in 1ml, 10 units in 1ml, 100 units in 1ml	Flush weekly when not in use, plus on completion of drug administration or blood sampling EXCEPT Vascuport: Flush monthly when not in use	1

DOSE

N.B. Suggested dose is an individual dose unless otherwise stated

DRUG Indication	Route	Times per day	0–4 weeks	4 weeks to 2 years	2–12 years	12 years and over	Availability	Comments	Dose ref
HYOSCINE HYDROBROMIDE Endotracheal secretion	Topical	Every 3 days			Half a patch (Not recommended <10 years)	One patch	Self-adhesive patch: 1.5mg hyoscine	Max. effect achieved 5–6 hours after applying first patch. Apply patch at a frequency determined by symptom control. Do not cut patch – for half a patch, mask the area not required. Experience suggests that more than the recommended dose is tolerated in 2–12 year age group	3
	SC/IV	Continuous			60–100µg/kg/day		Injection: 400µg in 1ml	Compatible with diamorphine at all usual concentrations. Physically compatible with morphine in syringe ± other drugs	4
KETAMINE Neuropathic pain	IV	Continuous		The effective dose is probably in the range 0.1–0.3mg/kg/hour but doses of 0.008–1.5mg/kg/hour have been used in children			Injection: 10mg in 1ml, 50mg in 1ml, 100mg in 1ml	This use of ketamine is not well established and the effective dose in individual patients may be outside the range quoted	5

DRUG Indication	Route	Times per day	<1 year	1–5 years	5–10 years	>10 years	Availability		Dose ref
LACTULOSE Constipation	Oral	2	2.5ml	5ml	10ml	15ml	Liquid		3

DRUG	Indication	Route	Times per day	DOSE — N.B. Suggested dose is an individual dose unless otherwise stated				Availability	Comments	Dose ref
				0–4 weeks	4 weeks to 2 years	2–12 years	12 years and over			
LORAZEPAM	Seizures	Sublingual Rectal IV			50/100µg/kg		4mg	Solution (SP): 2mg in 1ml. Injection: 4mg in 1ml	No licensed sublingual preparation available in UK	5
MIDAZOLAM	Sedation	SC/IV infusion	Continuous	Maintenance: 250–1000µg/kg/**day**. Always commence treatment at the lower end of the dose range, and exercise particular care if the patient is receiving concurrent opiate analgesia				Injection: 10mg in 2ml, 10mg in 5ml	Starting doses are quoted: increase as necessary to achieve effect. Compatible with diamorphine at all usual concentrations. No information on in-syringe compatibility with morphine, although frequently used without problem	1
MORPHINE SULPHATE	Analgesic	Oral/ Rectal	3–4 hourly	80µg/kg	200–400µg/kg		10–15mg	Syrup: 10mg in 5ml, 100mg in 5ml. Unit dose, 5ml oral vials: 10mg, 30mg, 100mg. Tablet: 10mg, 20mg. Sustained-release tablets: 5, 10, 15, 30, 60, 100 and 200mg Sachets: 20mg, 30mg. Suppositories: 5, 10, 15 and 30mg	Always adjust dosage to the needs of the patient – starting doses are given. Dose increments should be 30–50%, according to the patient's condition. Patients requiring sustained-release tablets may be stabilised on a syrup formulation, and the same total daily dose given as tablets in two divided doses OR the patient may be started on a sustained-release preparation. Increase dose of sustained-release preparation rather than frequency	3

DRUG	Indication	Route	Times per day	DOSE N.B. Suggested dose is an individual dose unless otherwise stated				Availability	Comments	Dose ref
				0–4 weeks	4 weeks to 2 years	2–12 years	12 years and over			
MORPHINE SULPHATE	Analgesic	IV	Single dose	100–200µg/kg			2.5–10mg	Injection: 10mg in 1ml, 15mg in 1ml, 20mg in 1ml, 30mg in 1ml	Compatible at 1mg/ml with cyclizine <2mg/ml. No information available on compatibility with haloperidol, hyoscine or methotrimeprazine	3
		SC/IV infusion	Continuous	10–30µg/kg/hour **OR** ½ the total daily oral dose over 24 hours. Use lower end of the dose range if <6 months						3
		Rectal	2	Oral dose of MST tablets				See Oral	MST tablets may be administered rectally when other routes are inappropriate or unavailable. Give same dose as per oral route but assess need for dose modification since bioavailability is very variable	5
ONDANSETRON	Anti-emetic	Oral	2–3		1–2mg	2–4mg	8mg	Tablet: 4mg, 8mg. Liquid: 4mg in 5ml	Twice daily dosing may be adequate	1
		IV	2–3		5mg/m2 or oral dose for age			Injection: 2mg in 1ml	Visually compatible with diamorphine. Physically compatible with morphine in syringe ± other drugs	1, 3
PARALDEHYDE	Anticonvulsant	Rectal	Single dose	0.3mg/kg (maximum dose: 10ml)			10ml	Injection: 5ml, 10ml	For uncontrolled fits. For rectal administration may be mixed with an equal volume of arachis or olive oil. Administer immediately if using a plastic syringe	3

DRUG	Indication	Route	Times per day	DOSE N.B. Suggested dose is an individual dose unless otherwise stated					Availability	Comments	Dose ref
				0–4 weeks	4 weeks to 2 years	2–12 years	12 years and over				
SODIUM CITRATE OSMOTIC LAXATIVE (Relaxit)		Rectal	Single dose			5ml			Single dose with nozzle: 5ml	Insert only half the nozzle length in children aged <3 years	2
TRANEXAMIC ACID Antifibrinolytic		Oral	3			25mg/kg			Tablet: 500mg Syrup: 500mg in 5ml	Use for mucosal bleeding in the presence of thrombocytopenia	3
		Topical	prn			Soak swab or gauze with injection solution and apply topically			Injection: 100mg in 1ml		1

Dose references

1. Local policy, Haematology and Oncology Departments, Birmingham Children's Hospital NHS Trust

2. *British National Formulary (BNF) 45 March 2003*. British Medical Association and Royal Pharmaceutical Society of Great Britain, London

3. Royal College of Paediatrics and Child Health, London (1999) *Medicines for Children*. 1st edn. RCPCH, London

4. Goldman A (Ed) (1994) *Care of the Dying Child*. Oxford University Press, Oxford

5. Other source/Reference on file

Notes on the administration of opiate drugs

Dosage equivalence

⌘ The potency of oral diamorphine and morphine is approximately half that of the same drugs given parenterally. Thus the oral dose will be twice that of the subcutaneous/intravenous (SC/IV) dose. However, it cannot be assumed that this will be appropriate in every patient, and dose should always be titrated against response.

⌘ Parenteral morphine is two-thirds as potent as parenteral diamorphine. Therefore 3mg IV morphine is equivalent to 2mg IV diamorphine.

⌘ Patients transferring from oral morphine in liquid form to a sustained-release preparation should be given the same total daily dose of the latter in two divided doses. The first dose of the sustained-release preparation should be given at the same time as the last dose of the liquid.

⌘ There is no therapeutic justification for changing patients from morphine to diamorphine, as both are equally effective analgesics. The difference is potency does not mean a difference in efficacy. The major difference is their solubility in aqueous media — diamorphine, with its much greater solubility, is most appropriate for SC use, particularly by infusion.

⌘ When changing from oral to SC/IV infusion, start diamorphine at a daily equivalent of one-third the current oral intake of oral morphine.

SC/IV administration

Diamorphine and morphine are compatible with Water for Injection, Sodium Chloride 0.9% and Dextrose 5%, and with any combination of the last two in this list, eg. Dextrose 4%/Sodium Chloride 0.18%. Check with pharmacy if compatibility with other diluents is required. Dilution is not critical, and may be determined by the equipment available and the patient's comfort, eg. maintenance of the infusion site.

Diamorphine is compatible for twenty-four hours in a syringe with cyclizine, haloperidol, hydrocortisone, hyoscine and methotrimeprazine. Stability data for such combinations are extremely limited after twenty-four hours. The corresponding data for morphine are generally not available. However, when mixing two or more drugs in a syringe, ALWAYS check for physical compatibility by looking closely for precipitation or colour change before the infusion is started, and at intervals while it is running. NOTE: Lack of precipitation or colour change etc. DOES NOT mean that the mixture is stable. Please check with pharmacy if in doubt.

April 2003

PALLIATIVE CARE
EQUIPMENT CASE CONTENTS

Drug (generic name)	Brand name	Strength	Quantity
Crotamiton	Eurax cream		1 x 30g
Cyclizine injection	Valoid	50 mg in 1 ml	5 x 1ml
Cyclizine suppositories		25 mg	1 x 12 NB. Fridge item
Dexamethasone		4 mg in 1 ml	5 x 1ml
Diazepam	Stesolid Rectal Tubes	5 mg	5 x 1ml
Glycerin suppositories		1g (Infant)	12 x 1g
Glycerin suppositories		2 g (Child)	12 x 2g
Haloperidol		5 mg in 1 ml	10 x 1ml
Heparin	Hepsal	50 units in 5 ml	10 x 5ml
Hyoscine injection		400 µg in 1ml	10 x 1ml
Hyoscine topical patch	Scopoderm	1.5 mg	1
Methotrimeprazine	Nozinan	25 mg in 1ml	10 x 1ml
Midazolam	Hypnovel	10 mg in 2ml	10 x 2ml
Ondansetron	Zofran	4 mg in 2ml	5 x 2ml
Sodium Citrate Compound Enema	Relaxit Micro-enema		4
Sodium Chloride		0.9%	4 x 10 ml
Streptokinase		250,000 units	1
Water for Injection			4 x 10 ml

Syringe Driver Prescription Sheet

COMMUNITY PRESCRIPTION SHEET

NAME OF PATIENT: ....

DOB: ....

ADDRESS: ....
....
....
....

HOSPITAL NUMBER: ....

MOST RECENT WEIGHT: .... CONSULTANT: ....

Please infuse the following drugs:

1. Diamorphine

2. ....

3. ....

as a 24-hour infusion subcutaneously/intravenously via syringe driver.

Make total 24-hour volume to .... ml with Water for Injection.

Increase diamorphine by .... mg (............................. milligrams)
if necessary to control pain.

Other instructions:

SIGNED: .... NAME: ....

DATE: ....

6

Practical considerations in paediatric palliative care

The transition from palliative to terminal care raises a wide range of issues for the family. Adams and Deveau (1988) summarise this period as a time when families strive to find the balance between maintaining hope and facing death, while acknowledging that they have done all they can for their child. Feelings of anger and sadness may predominate as they face a situation over which they have no control. At this time the health professional can provide not only practical assistance, but also reassurance and support. The palliative phase may last for a few weeks or many months. The diversity in palliative care necessitates individualised planning that meets the needs of the child and family. The majority of children are happiest in their own home, and this is usually the location of choice for the child and family as death approaches (see *Chapter 2*).

This chapter will examine the impact of culture on the practical organisation of palliative care in the home setting and arrangement of the funeral.

Discussions with family

It is not possible to completely prepare parents for the death of their child. Yet it is important to ensure that they have the information they require to enable them to care for their child at home. It is difficult to determine how much information to give parents or guardians at any one time; the decision is gauged on the family's response to initial discussions and the time span deemed available for imparting the information. Some families prefer to know all about the symptoms that may occur and how it is anticipated their child will die, whereas others want only to address current symptom control issues. Not all children slip into a coma and die peacefully. It is important to inform parents of potentially distressing symptoms that could occur, such as convulsions or haemorrhage, so that they can be instructed on what action might be needed. The timing of the discussion requires careful consideration. Pre-emptive measures can help to minimise the helplessness felt by parents caring for children with such symptoms; conversely, imparting information prematurely may leave the family worrying about the likelihood of their child developing the symptom.

Parents may have great fears about how their child might die, but not be able to verbalise this to the healthcare professional. Although it is not possible to give the family a clear prognosis in terms of weeks, the skilled healthcare professional may be able to recognise when the child has only days to live: the respiratory rate may fall, with the breathing becoming shallower, and Cheyne-Stokes respiration may develop. The child may become pale and their extremities cool. Clear explanations of the signs, their significance and treatment should be given, empowering parents in practical care. This information can enable the family to make important decisions, such as informing siblings of the impending death or arranging for extended family to visit.

Communication is covered in more detail in *Chapter 4*.

Practical care

Providing continuous care for a sick child twenty-four hours a day can leave parents physically and emotionally exhausted. Parents may be frightened to leave their child's side in case he/she dies, and in so doing stop looking after themselves. Regular eating and drinking patterns are often forgotten. Strategies to help parents at this time should be discussed. Often the family is affected through disruptions to normal routines. Everyday issues, such as taking the other children to school, shopping or providing meals, become difficult.

For some, a close network of family and friends address these issues instinctively, but other socially isolated families can find themselves in an almost impossible position. In these cases it may be appropriate to identify agencies that could provide assistance, such as night sitters or linking with a children's hospice. Some agencies can be of only limited use to families, because of the need for staff to have a police check undertaken. Police checking involves undertaking a criminal record check for the person concerned, identifying whether any convictions are held on the national police computer or local police records. A police check is required for all posts involving contact with children. The main difficulties identified in arranging police checks are payment for the process of police checking, and the time taken for this process to be completed.

It is important to reassess the family's wishes regularly in order to identify and address what is important for them. Visits from healthcare professionals should be openly planned with the family to meet the needs of the child and family, and not those of the healthcare professional.

Overview of care of the child

⌘ **Hygiene**: Assistance with bathing/washing may be needed, particularly with an older or immobile child. Assessment for aids within the house may be necessary, and the occupational therapist should be involved. The importance of regular mouth care and treatment of infections, such as oral *Candida*, should be discussed with the family. Children may find soft toothbrushes or sponge sticks more comfortable to use than their normal toothbrush. Correct positioning of the child and pressure area care need to be explained and demonstrated.

⌘ **Nutrition**: Many concerns are raised when the child's ability to eat or drink becomes affected. Feeder cups and straws may help some children; others may already be using artificial feeding methods such as nasogastric feeds. Families need to be shown how to help keep their child comfortable if they are unable to eat or drink in the terminal phase of their illness. This can be achieved through gentle mouth care with sponge sticks and water, and the use of moisturising cream or salve to the lips.

⌘ **Stimulation and diversion**: This is guided by the child's preferences: for example, play, listening to tapes/stories, and watching videos should be encouraged. Families also need to be informed of the importance of continuing to involve the child, even when he/she is in a coma and not able to respond. Listening to tapes or favourite stories may be comforting not only to the child, but also to the family, who can be practically involved in reading the story.

⌘ **Ambience**: The optimal level of light, noise and comfort will vary from family to family. What is right for one family may not suit another, and each family should be supported in their decisions, provided that they do not adversely affect the child. Sometimes the geography of a house is re-arranged, such as moving the bed downstairs, enabling the child to be in the midst of family life throughout the day.

Aids and adaptations

For some children, disease progression is linked with increasing disability and consequent loss of independence. The effect of the loss of physical ability on the child and family is immeasurable. Children may experience:

- Motor problems   – reduced mobility
       – paralysis
       – ataxia
       – generalised weakness
       – loss of head control
- Incontinence   – urinary
       – faecal
- Communication   – dysphasia
  difficulties   – aphasia
       – deafness
- Eating problems   – difficulty in chewing and swallowing
       – drooling

A well child may become severely disabled within a short period of time. However, the specific timescale will depend on the cause:

⌘ Spinal cord compression may be associated with rapid onset of symptoms.
⌘ Brain and spinal cord tumours/metastases are associated with gradual loss of function.

The psychological and emotional effects of loss of ability are immense. Young children may regress in new-found skills, such as dressing themselves, and also in their behaviour and language. The period of adolescence can be particularly distressing for the older child who becomes physically dependent upon parents (see *Chapter 7*).

Research has shown that families are not always fully informed of the practical aids available to assist them in providing care in the home (Doyle, 1994; O'Neill and Rodway, 1998). Provision of equipment within the home varies between health authorities, and local directories have been compiled in some areas. Community nurses are able to access equipment such as bath seats, commodes, bed rails and electrical beds. Basic pressure-relieving mattresses and chair cushions can also be provided, but if pressure area care is a potential problem it is advisable to liaise with the tissue viability nurse for advice. He/ she has access to a range of pressure-relieving mattresses and beds that can be rented.

In some circumstances, an occupational therapist may be involved in an assessment of the home. Occupational therapy focuses on helping people with everyday activities. By undertaking a home assessment, the occupational therapist can recommend the best equipment, aids and adaptations, such as wheelchairs, bathroom layout and handrails.

The physiotherapist can help with mobility issues, such as organising wheelchairs, and teaching the child and family correct lifting and/or transfer techniques. This is important, as in many cases the parents are the main care givers and a lack of knowledge of correct lifting techniques can result in injury.

Financial support

The period of palliative care may follow many months or years of children undergoing treatment. This can have a huge impact on the family dynamics, as the family routine is thrown into turmoil with unanticipated hospital admissions. Finances can be strained as parents choose to spend time with their child, and work becomes a low priority. Grants for families fulfilling set criteria are available from organisations such as CLIC-Sargent Cancer Care for Children, The Family Fund Trust, (see *Appendix 2*). Information pertinent to each specific area will be available from local CLIC-Sargent social workers or specialist practitioners.

Disability Living Allowance (DLA) is a benefit for children who have a serious illness or disability and require more help and care than other children of the same age. Terminally ill children, ie. those expected to die within six months as a result of their disease (George, 2000), can automatically claim for a higher rate DLA. A DS1500 form needs to be completed by the GP or consultant. The Benefits Agency aims to clear these claims within ten working days (see *Appendix 2* for further information).

CLIC-Sargent Cancer Care for Children

This is an independent charity that aims to help families of a child with cancer with the emotional, practical and financial impact of the diagnosis and treatment. CLIC-Sargent-funded social workers, employed by local authority Social Services, are based at all of the major childhood cancer centres as well as in some of the smaller, outlying centres. They have a major role in offering information and access to practical support, such as addressing financial, child care or travel issues.

Holidays

Charities, such as CLIC-Sargent Cancer Care, and some wish foundations offer families of children with cancer the opportunity of a family holiday. In some cases this can be a special holiday (see *Appendix 1* for a list of organisations and contact numbers). Arranging travel insurance cover for these holidays can be difficult, but organisations such as Christian Lewis Children's Cancer Care can help to ensure that families obtain insurance against any eventuality.

Taking controlled drugs abroad

Up to fifteen days' worth of opioids can usually be taken abroad without licence from the Home Office. For more than fifteen days, or if the dose is high, it is recommended that:

⌘ The family should obtain a letter from the prescribing doctor stating that the medicines are prescribed for personal use.

⌘ The embassy for the country being visited should be contacted to ascertain their regulations for taking the medicine into the country.

⌘ The Medicines Control Agency should be contacted to ascertain whether an export certificate will be required (Tel: 020 7273 3000).

⌘ Customs and excise should be contacted to ascertain labelling and packaging requirements (Tel: 0845 010 9000).

⌘ The Home Office should be contacted to ascertain whether a licence is required. (Tel: London 020 7273 3530; Leeds 011 3220 4570). Ten days should be allowed for processing the licence if required (Faull *et al*, 1998).

For further information, see *Appendix 3*.

Religious and cultural issues

Healthcare professionals may experience communication difficulties in caring for some ethnic minority families, particularly outside office hours when the interpreting services are not so readily available. Firth (2001) acknowledged this problem in her study and found that initiatives to improve advocacy, link worker and interpreter schemes were underused or inadequate. There is an acknowledged lack of accessible written information available in a range of languages.

Hill and Penso (1995) researched access to adult specialist palliative care services by black and ethnic minority groups. These groups were found not to utilise hospice and palliative care services in relation to their numbers. The research identified the need for palliative care services to provide care that was sensitive to the cultural needs of the individual, in particular linguistic, religious, spiritual and dietary needs.

The importance of religions and rituals in palliative care and at the time of death should be respected. Healthcare professionals should seek to adhere to family preferences at all times. Conflicts can occur with gender issues, beliefs about death and pain control. Difficulties in understanding cultural and religious beliefs affect not only healthcare professionals but also second- or third-generations families, who may need to turn to their parents or grandparents for guidance at such times.

It is not the intention to extensively detail here the impact of different religions on palliative care and funeral arrangements, but literature (Neuberger, 1994) is available and should be made accessible to healthcare professionals within the workplace.

Organ donation

Following or before the death of their child, families may request information on organ donation. Retrieval of tissues must be carried out within twenty-four hours of the death. For children dying of cancer, only corneal donation is feasible. The donated corneas are used to restore sight in patients with diseased or opaque corneas. Scleral tissue can also be used to hold a false eye. For children dying of leukaemia or lymphoma, no organs at all can be donated (Council of Europe, 1997).

For further information, the National Tissue Donor Coordinator can be contacted on pager 07693 086823.

At the time of death

When preparing a family for the death of their child it is helpful to inform the family about what to do at the time of death. However, not all families reach the point of being able to discuss this. For these families it may be appropriate to leave written information and contact numbers in an envelope. Useful numbers may include the GP and community nurse daytime and out-of-hours contact numbers.

KEY POINTS

◆ The family does not need to contact anyone immediately after the child dies unless they feel that they would like to speak to a healthcare professional, or have one visit.

◆ They should be encouraged to spend as much time together as a family as they wish.

◆ When they feel ready, they will need to contact their GP, who will certify the death.

Provided that the doctor has seen the child within fourteen days of the death, he/she can issue the Notification of Death certificate. If the child has not been seen within this time period, the GP will need to speak to the coroner. In the majority of cases of childhood cancer the coroner will instruct the GP to issue the Notification of Death certificate. If the death occurs outside normal working hours, a deputising doctor may attend. In this case, the attending, deputising doctor can certify the death and then inform the child's GP, who can then issue the Notification of Death certificate (provided that he/she has seen the child within the previous fourteen days).

At the point of death a family may want to have a short blessing or ceremony for their child, even if they are not religious. The child's body can remain in the house until the funeral, in which case guidance should be sought from the funeral director on caring for the body. The family may wish to take photographs or a lock of hair; however, for the Muslim or Sikh family it is important that the hair is not cut after death. Families may wish to wash and dress their child, and should be advised to lie their child flat with one pillow beneath the head. Practising Muslim, Hindu and Jewish families usually attend to the body themselves and carry out traditional rituals.

Immediately after the child dies there is general muscle flaccidity, usually followed by a period of partial or total rigidity (rigor mortis), which passes off as the signs of decomposition appear (Knight, 1991). Rigor mortis occurs between thirty minutes and six hours after death, most commonly between two and four hours, and progresses for up to nine hours, by which time it is fully established. After thirty-six to forty-eight hours it begins to wear off and the muscles relax. Rigor mortis is a result of a biochemical reaction leading to a reduction in the muscle store of glycogen, and will therefore progress more quickly in a heated room. If the body remains very cold, rigor may persist indefinitely (Marshall, 1976). Informing the family about rigor mortis is important for those families who may choose to dress their child and find that they are not be able to manipulate the limbs.

Case study 6.1

Laura, aged six years, died at home on Good Friday from a nasopharyngeal rhabdomyosarcoma. The tumour had extended from her nose onto her face. Her parents wanted to keep her body at home until the funeral, which, due to the Bank Holiday period, was planned for seven days later. Laura's body changed quickly and the discharge from the visible tumour was distressing to the family.

The funeral director was approached, who sensitively discussed the care of Laura's body and advised embalming. Parents agreed on the understanding that her father carried her in his arms from the house to the funeral director's car, and that she would be returned to the house by the end of the afternoon. The funeral director was able to meet these requests. The care, respect, gentleness and support shown to the family were greatly appreciated.

Apart from nasogastric tubes, which can be removed relatively easily, it is best to seek advice from the funeral directors about the removal of other tubes or lines such as central venous catheters, as profuse bleeding can still occur after death.

During the child's illness, equipment and medication often accumulate within the house. Communication with the family will elicit how quickly they wish the equipment to be removed from the house after the death. Drugs, including controlled drugs, can be returned to any pharmacy. The family should be advised to arrange for this to be completed at their earliest opportunity.

Case study 6.1 demonstrates the ways in which a family's wishes can be met. In this scenario the funeral directors listened to the wishes of the family and gently guided them in their decision-making.

Dominica (1987) describes the beneficial impact on the acceptance of death that can occur if the family maintains close contact with their dead child. The dead child may appear peaceful in the initial few hours after death, but after two or three days the visual changes leave families feeling that he/she no longer looks like their child.

If the child dies in hospital, provided that there is no coroner's referral or hospital post-mortem, the family can take their child's body home. Whittle and Cutts (2002) highlight that parents may not be aware that they can take their child's body home, and that the nurses and doctors involved may not raise the subject through their own lack of bknowledge of the organisation involved.

The family will need to complete the relevant paperwork before leaving the hospital; the forms differ from hospital to hospital. They should also be advised on how to register the death, and be given a contact number for personnel who will be able to answer any queries (Whittle and Cutts, 2002). Written information is preferable to verbal instructions, which are often forgotten.

The services of a funeral director may be required for the transportation home, although the family can take their child's body home in their own car if they prefer. Involvement of the funeral director is recommended with the older or heavier child, who may be difficult to carry, or where there is a risk of leaking body fluids, which can prove very distressing to the unprepared family.

Post-mortem

For the majority of children dying from cancer, a post-mortem will not be required. Legally, a death is referred to the county coroner if:

- the child dies suddenly or unexpectedly
- the death occurred in unusual circumstances
- the doctors are unaware of the cause of death
- the child has undergone surgery during the previous twenty-four hours.

For some families, such as Orthodox Jews, a post-mortem is not acceptable. It is hoped that in these circumstances the coroner would be sensitive to the beliefs of the family, and contribute to discussions with the family and rabbi (Neuberger, 1994).

Registering the death

Registration of a death must occur within five days, unless the coroner is involved. The family may find it helpful for an appointment to be made for them to attend the office of the Registration of Births, Marriages and Deaths; for other families, details of office location and opening hours may be sufficient. The family may choose to nominate a relative or friend to register the death for them.

The person registering the death should be one of the following:

- a relative
- a person present at the death
- an occupant of the house where the death occurred
- the organiser of the funeral but not the funeral director.

The funeral directors may be able to assist with transport to the office if this poses a problem to the family.

The registrar will need to know:

- the date and place of birth and death
- the full name of the deceased
- the home address of the deceased
- parents' full names, places and dates of birth, home addresses and occupations.

The registrar will also require:

- notification of death certificate
- NHS medical card
- benefit or allowance books.

The registrar will take the Notification of Death form from the family. They will be issued with a green certificate (Disposal Certificate) and a white certificate (BD8). The Disposal Certificate enables the funeral director to complete arrangements for burial and cremation to take place, and the BD8 has to be completed and sent to the Department for Work and Pensions (formerly Department of Social Security) for the area where the death occurred.

Copies of the Entry of Death (known as the death certificate) may be purchased from the registrar and may be required for formalities such as closing bank accounts.

Relatives do not have to go to the location where the death occurred to register the death. They can give the information to any registrar in England or Wales and have the details sent to the register office for the district in which the death occurred, where these will be registered. This is referred to as Registration by Declaration. The registrar for the district where the death occurred will post the certificates to the family. This may take a few days and could cause a delay in the organisation of the funeral. The funeral director should be informed if this is the family's intent.

Arranging a funeral

Arranging a funeral can be very stressful, as families strive to provide a special personal memorial.

Choosing a funeral director may be difficult. The family may wish to meet the funeral director before the child's death, but generally this is done afterwards. The funeral director will listen to the family's wishes and discuss the structure of the service they require. It may be that the child has already planned his/her own funeral, or discussed funerals or cremations. The service offered by funeral directors varies, as do the charges. Many do not charge for their services, only for the fees paid out on the families' behalf, such as crematorium fees. The family will be given a written estimate of the costs of the funeral. Funeral directors may offer different payment options to help families meet the costs. A funeral usually takes place within a day to a fortnight of the death, depending on religious beliefs, family wishes and administrative issues. Muslim families, however, will hold the funeral within twenty-four hours of the death.

Should the family wish to keep the body at home, the funeral director can advise. As a general principle, the room should be kept as cool as possible, with heaters and radiators turned off. Windows should be kept closed to reduce the risk of flies entering the room. The funeral director can prepare the body for the family, washing and dressing the child and closing his/her eyes. In some cases, embalming may be advised: the body is taken away for a few hours and treated to maintain a natural look for as long as possible, and then returned to the family home. An indication that this may be necessary is the nail bed turning black, which can occur within a few days after death. Any such deterioration is irreversible and may prove very upsetting to the family. Embalming may need to be discussed with the family in the immediate period after death.

Should the family wish the body to be taken to the Chapel of Rest at the funeral directors, this can be arranged at a time to suit the family. They can then visit, as they desire. In many Chapels of Rest, lower trestles are used so that the body is at the correct height for siblings, and Moses baskets may be used for babies. A variety of children's coffins are available, including a selection with pictures on the sides, such as rainbows or balloons.

It is important to prepare siblings and family members for seeing the body, eg. by informing children that their brother or sister will feel cold to the touch, which can be distressing to the unprepared. Children can be encouraged to take drawings or writing in, to be placed in the coffin or attached to the outside. This gives them an opportunity to say goodbye. The family should be encouraged to do what they feel is right for them.

Cremation

Approximately 70% of all recorded deaths in Great Britain are followed by cremation. Orthodox Jews and Muslims do not allow cremation, but it is accepted by all Christian denominations, Sikhs, Hindus, Parsees and Buddhists (Dignity Funerals Limited, undated). Two components of the cremation form require completion. The doctor who issues the death notice usually completes the first part of the form and nominates a colleague to complete the second part. The nominated doctor would clarify information through a telephone conversation with the first doctor before carrying out an external examination of the body and completing the second part of the form. The doctors charge a fee for completing the forms. In some cases the funeral director is asked to approach a doctor to complete the second part of the form.

Funeral directors are unable to undertake any preparation, embalming or placing of the body in a coffin until the two forms are completed.

It is preferred that jewellery is removed before cremation takes place, but some families request that it remains with their child. It is common practice for toys or mementoes to be placed with the child in the coffin, but in order to comply with the 1990 Environmental Protection Act, man-made materials such as PVC, metals and glass cannot be put into the coffin (Dignity Funerals Limited, undated). These issues should be discussed with the funeral director.

The cremation ceremony

The mourners generally congregate at the crematorium in the waiting area or entrance. When the coffin arrives, the principal mourners follow it into the chapel, followed by everyone else. Crematoria usually allocate thirty-minute periods for the service, but two or more time slots can be requested if required. The service can follow a traditional religious theme or be from a non-religious perspective, eg. a humanist service, and can be held at the crematorium or at a local place of worship. Following the service the committal of the body takes place and the coffin is usually obscured from view by curtains or withdrawn from the chapel. At this point the nameplate is checked by the crematorium staff, to ensure correct identity. The coffin and its contents are placed in a cremator, which produces very intense heat. The process takes about ninety minutes. The remaining calcined bones and any metals such as implants are removed from the cremator, cooled, and placed in a machine that reduces the bone to a granular consistency. These are then transferred to a final container. With a young infant, there may be no collectable remains and families should be informed of this. The cremation usually takes place within a few hours of the service. Each cremator is only large enough to take one coffin.

The ashes are given to the family or kept by the crematorium or funeral director until the family have decided what they would like to do with them. The ashes can be scattered or buried in a garden of remembrance or be kept in a place that is special to the family. If the family wishes to disperse the ashes anywhere else, then the permission of the landowner should be sought. A funeral director can arrange for the ashes to be sent to another part of the UK or abroad, should this be required.

Some families choose to have an additional ceremony for the internment of the ashes.

The crematorium may hold a Book of Remembrance or the family may chose to have a plaque in the grounds. The crematorium staff can advise families.

Cremation is less expensive than burial and charges may vary according to the age of the child.

Burial

For some religions, burial is the only option. Muslims and Orthodox Jews are always buried. Hindu adults are cremated, but young Hindu children and infants may be buried or cremated.

The funeral director can approach either the minister of the church if burial in the churchyard is requested, or the cemetery to see if room is available. Many local church graveyards are now full and have strict local rules regarding memorials. The cemeteries are owned by the local council and can provide a baby plot or adult plot. A child can be buried in an adult plot with a view to the parent being buried there too, but this decision needs to be made before the service so that a deeper hole can be dug. Alternatively, adjacent plots can be purchased. It is also possible to bury your child on private land, but permission must be obtained from the local council. Regulations exist as to the type of memorial stones accepted in the local churchyard or cemetery and the wording that can be used. The funeral director or monumental mason can advise the family on this issue.

Costs vary and include burial, church and minister costs.

The burial ceremony

The ceremony can be religious, conducted by the family's own religious leader or one recommended by the funeral director, or non-religious. It can be held in almost any venue, even at home. The funeral director can advise whether permission is required. The ceremony allows the family and friends to come together in remembrance of the child and offers support to the immediate family.

The format generally comprises songs, hymns, music, readings and poems. A recording of the service may provide solace to the family at a later date, especially if they were too distraught to remember the actual service. An order of service, often with a photograph of the child, provides a tangible memory for the mourners.

Families may question whether siblings should attend the service. This decision should rest with the family, but they should be reassured that children are usually helped in their grieving if involved in both the arrangements and the service itself (see *Chapter 4* for further information).

Memorials

Cemeteries adhere to local regulations as to when a gravestone can be erected, but as a general rule this occurs approximately six months after the burial. The headstone can be engraved to the family's request, with pictures such as teddies or words. Enamel photoplaques are also available.

Repatriation

A family may wish to take the body of their child back to their home country, be that from England to Scotland or Ireland or further afield. This is known as repatriation. The Registrar of Births, Marriages and Deaths would inform the coroner of the family's intent. The family would not receive the green Disposal Certificate but will be given an 'Out of England' form by the Coroner's Office. This can usually be collected within a few hours of registration. The family will need to obtain at least two copies of the death certificate when they register the death. The funeral director will require a copy of the original death certificate and the 'Out of England' certificate. Some countries may require an embalming *care*

and/or a 'Free from infection' letter or certificate. The latter would provided by the GP or hospital consultant. Families may then make e transportation arrangements. If the body is to be transported by aeroplane, a zinc-lined coffin is required. The zinc lining can be removed on arrival at the destination if required. Repatriation costs are often high.

Bereavement

For the families of a child diagnosed with a life-threatening illness such as cancer, the grieving process often starts at the point of diagnosis, with grief for the loss of the healthy child. However grim the given prognosis, families report feeling hope right up until the point of death. At this time the family become embroiled in funeral arrangements. Often it is not until after the funeral that the full impact of what has happened is realised, combined with overwhelming physical and emotional exhaustion.

Grieving is a normal response to an adverse event and most families do not require specialist intervention (Association for Children with Life-threatening or Terminal Conditions and their Families [ACT] and the Royal College of Paediatrics and Child Health [RCPCH], 1997). There is no right or wrong way to grieve – everyone reacts differently. Partners may grieve differently and at a different rate, and may need reassurance that this is normal.

A minority of parents suffer an abnormal grief reaction, and for them specialist help is available through referral to a bereavement counsellor, psychotherapist, clinical psychologist or psychiatrist.

Effective communication between the healthcare professionals involved in the care of the child is essential for clarifying roles in the bereavement care of the family. Contact is usually maintained with the family for a minimum of 2 years, through letters, telephone calls and visits (see *Appendix 4* for the West Midlands Paediatric Macmillan Team's bereavement policy).

Summary

A coordinated approach is required for effective organisation of the practical care of the child dying within the family home. A key worker should be identified to link with all the healthcare professionals and establish functional communication pathways.

Through discussions with the family, practical assistance that is required, or perceived to be required in the future, can be identified and implemented wherever feasible. The implications of cultural issues for the provision of both palliative and bereavement care should be acknowledged and respected.

References

Adams DW, Deveau EJ (1988) *Coping with Childhood Cancer: Where do we go from here?* Kinbridge Publications, Hamilton, Ontario

Association for Children with Life-threatening or Terminal Conditions and their Families (ACT) and the Royal College of Paediatrics and Child Health (RCPCH) (1997) *A Guide to the Development of Children's Palliative Care Services.* ACT/RCPCH, London

Council of Europe (1997) *International Consensus Document: Standardisation of Organ Screening to Prevent Transmission of Neoplastic Disease.* Transplant Newsletter June 1997; 2i: 4–10

Dignity Funerals Limited (Undated) Family information booklets. Dignity Funerals Limited, Sutton Coldfield

Dominica F (1987) Reflections on death in childhood. *Br Med J* **294**: 108–10

Doyle D (1994) *Domiciliary Palliative Care: A guide for the primary health care team.* Oxford University Press, Oxford

Faull C, Carter Y, Woof R (1998) *Handbook of Palliative Care.* Blackwell Science, London

Firth S (2001) *Wider Horizons: Care of the Dying in a Multicultural Society.* National Council for Hospice and Specialist Palliative Care Services, London

George C (2000) *Welfare Benefits Handbook 2000/2001.* Child Poverty Action Group, London

Hill D, Penso D (1995) *Opening Doors: Improving access to hospice and specialist palliative care services by members of the black and minority ethnic communities.* Occasional Paper 7. National Council for Hospice and Specialist Palliative Care Services, London

Knight B (1991) *Forensic Pathology.* Edward Arnold, London

Marshall TK (1976) Changes after death. In: Camps F, Robinson A, Lucas B (Eds). *Gradwohl's Legal Medicine.* 3rd edn. John Wright and Sons Ltd, Bristol

Neuberger J (1994) *Caring for Dying People of Different Faiths.* 2nd edn. Mosby, London

O'Neill B, Rodway A (1998) ABC of Palliative Care: Care in the community. *Br Med J* **316**: 373–7

Whittle M, Cutts S (2002) Time to go home: assisting families to take their child home following a planned hospital or hospice death. *Paediatr Nurs* **14**(10): 24–8

7

Challenges in providing palliative care to adolescents

Adolescence is widely accepted as a challenging phase of development (Heiney *et al*, 1990; Chambas, 1991). The struggle for both independence and intimacy are central themes of this period (Reres, 1980). The resolution of these conflicts occurs at a time of physical, mental and social change. Establishing identity and self-image, gaining autonomy from parents and developing a positive sexual role are issues that the adolescent is exposed to and required to master (Heiney *et al*, 1990; Grant and Roberts, 1998).

Illness is particularly threatening and poorly tolerated in adolescence (Thornes *et al*, 2001). It is therefore a difficult time to experience cancer and its effects (Copeland, 1998). The addition of a diagnosis of cancer can create an overwhelming degree of stress, with the adolescent being exposed to hair loss, weight gain/loss, invasive procedures, isolation from peer group, the threat of sterility and lack of privacy (Pinkerton *et al*, 1994). These combined stressors may result in some adolescents experiencing severe psychosocial problems (Ellis, 1991). The oncology fraternity have attempted to address the unique needs of adolescents through the establishment of dedicated adolescent units and designated teenage areas within paediatric wards (Hollis and Morgan, 2001).

Furthermore, for adolescents confronting death there are considerable multifaceted challenges, made more complex by their age. This chapter will consider these challenges, drawing on experience and evidence from the literature.

Physical dependence

For a teenager, becoming physically reliant upon parents, relatives and siblings can provoke feelings of embarrassment, uselessness and being a burden. A study of young people diagnosed with cancer (Enskar *et al*, 1997) highlights the distress that adolescents feel as a result of their dependence upon parents. At this stage of development, young people would normally be looking to establish independence (Ellis, 1991). Physical dependence, however, may obstruct their freedom and therefore compromise autonomy (Thornes *et al*, 2001).

Debilitating symptoms may prompt re-emergence of parental protectiveness, previously relinquished (Hinds *et al,* 1992). This phenomenon has been recognised during and following cancer treatment (Weekes and Kagan, 1994). In an attempt to help their sick adolescent, parents may encourage reliance and assume age-inappropriate responsibilities.

Case study 7.1

Kirsty was seventeen years old. She had always enjoyed an active social life and had an eighteen-year-old boyfriend. They liked to go to bars and clubs in town at the weekends. Kirsty's osteosarcoma was no longer curable. She was taking etoposide orally and was requiring weak opioids for pain. Her lung metastases caused some breathlessness. Kirsty still wanted to go clubbing but her mum refused to let her go. She was frightened that the smoky environment would harm her daughter. She was concerned that both Kirsty and her friends would abuse alcohol, that Kirsty might hurt herself, or that her peer group might not recognise that she was ill. The relationship between Kirsty and her mum deteriorated. Kirsty accused her mum of wanting her to die in misery with no fun. Kirsty's social worker spoke to them both and was able to achieve some resolution. Kirsty's boyfriend agreed to drive Kirsty to and from town, Kirsty agreed to stay clear of excessively smoke-filled environments, and mum agreed to give Kirsty some space. Kirsty got her freedom back. Her mum, however, remained agitated when Kirsty was with her friends. When Kirsty was too debilitated to leave the house, her mum guiltily confessed that she felt less stressed now that she knew where Kirsty was.

It is widely recognised that the central development task of the adolescent years is successful attainment of personal identity (Erickson, 1980). In *Case study 7.1,* Kirsty's identity is strongly associated with her peer group and their activities. Conflict arose when her mum tried to exert authority over Kirsty, threatening what had previously been Kirsty's social norm. Clearly, Kirsty wanted her life to remain as normal as possible. Her mum, understandably, wanted to protect her from any perceived danger or threat. Kirsty's mum was placed in an invidious position.

Professionals should recognise the difficulties that parents experience in allowing an appropriate level of autonomy for their adolescent. Nevertheless, as in *Case study 7.1,* parents should be encouraged to enable the teenager to be as independent as possible, even when his/her disease is debilitating (Fochtman, 1979; Heiney, 1989).

The disease process can prompt a shift in family dynamics as the young person becomes increasingly unwell and thus more dependent. Changes in roles should be recognised and acknowledged with family members (Roberts *et al,* 1998). The adolescent may feel that he/she has lost previous roles, while siblings may perceive that they are required to be more adult or that they have become care givers. The effects of such role changes on a family will be highly individual and subject to a variety of influences.

Social attitudes to a sibling undertaking physical care that will, by necessity, involve touching the teenager's body, in particular genitalia, may be negative. The implication is that the intimate care is seen in some way as 'dirty'. The family may themselves take this view or worry about the attitudes of relatives and friends. Such concerns may deter the sibling who wishes to be involved in this way, or may result in the family discouraging such intimate care. In contrast, some cultures consider it acceptable or even the norm for an older sibling to deliver such care. For example, among the Muslim community, administering physical care is considered a female role. If the mother is not around or has younger children, the care is likely to fall to older female siblings. Furthermore, the undertaking of physical care is considered an unacceptable role for a father.

The importance of privacy and dignity is magnified in the care of the adolescent, particularly in relation to appearance and hygiene (McCarthy, 1995). Thus incontinence, which can be a difficult issue at any age, may be particularly distressing for adolescents. Some may equate the necessary incontinence aids (nappies) and the need for such intimate care with a loss of dignity. Teenagers might perceive their incontinence as regression to a baby-like state or feel that this lack of control is inconsistent with their status as an adolescent. Parents, siblings and carers may in turn find such care difficult, both emotionally and physically (see *Case study 7.2*).

Case study 7.2

Samantha was a teenage girl with an incurable brain tumour. She was severely physically disabled by her disease and had limited ability to communicate. She was bed bound, needed help with all aspects of care and was also doubly incontinent. Despite difficulties with communication, she was able to articulate her displeasure at the need to wear nappies. In an attempt to make the situation less embarrassing, she and her family agreed that they would refer to them by a code name. Samantha's family cared for her at home with great skill and were able to adapt and cope with her deterioration. However, her mum talked frankly about the difficulties of cleaning Samantha after bowel actions because of her size and the fact that the faeces stuck to her pubic hair. She also talked of how difficult it was to keep Samantha clean during menstruation and how unpleasant this was for both her and Samantha. Together they decided that it was best for Samantha to commence the contraceptive pill and for her to take it continually to avoid menstrual bleeds.

Most people have experience of changing a baby's nappy. There are, however, huge differences when changing and cleaning an adolescent. The most obvious physical difficulties will be the potential size and weight of the young person. It is entirely possible that parents may not have seen their child's naked body for several years as it is usual for adolescents to be extremely body conscious and reluctant to allow others to see their physique. The bathroom and bedroom door are kept closed when bathing and changing and there is an often unspoken agreement that access is not permitted. Most will do all that is possible to protect their privacy. This may, however, be impossible within the context of needing physical care. The sick adolescent and parent will potentially have to confront the embarrassment and difficulties posed by pubic hair, menstruation or penile erection.

⌘ **Size/weight**: The physical size of the adolescent means that changing his/her nappy can present difficulties. The teenager may be near to or full adult height/weight and thus impossible for one person to lift. Although, theoretically, help is available from the community nursing staff, many parents, understandably, will not leave their child dirty until a visit is due.

⌘ **Pubic hair**: The presence of pubic hair can make cleaning after defecation a challenging process. Even with the use of wet wipes it may be difficult to remove all faeces successfully. This may therefore involve soap and water washing after each bowel action. When the adolescent is bed- or wheelchair-bound, this can involve considerable preparation and activity such as hoist, bed bath, bed changing and accessibility of bath.

⌘ **Menstruation**: This is an essentially personal experience. Although an open topic of conversation between many mothers and their teenage daughters, the practicalities of hygiene and the changing of sanitary products is something that is guided through discussion rather than done for the teenager. The necessity for this type of intimate care can be embarrassing. A parent's choice of sanitary product in this situation may not be what the adolescent is most comfortable with. The idea of inserting a tampon for someone else may be offensive. Furthermore, maintaining cleanliness, particularly during heavy menstruation, may be difficult.

⌘ **Penile erection**: The act of cleansing male genitalia may stimulate the penis, causing arousal. It is also common for men to wake in the morning with an erection. Although parents will be aware of these natural occurrences, it is unlikely that they have previously seen their son in such a potentially embarrassing situation. Likewise, undertaking catheter care for the adolescent can be equally awkward.

These additional physical issues not only present the practical problems illustrated, but also highlight the unrelenting and offensive nature of the disease process.

The specialist practitioner can help the patient and parents to discuss these issues openly. Professional willingness to introduce and debate such difficult subjects in a direct and candid manner will demonstrate normalisation of these issues. It may enable the family to be more open and frank in their own discussions and, in consequence, allow them to share their feelings. The use of the customary blunt language of adolescence can help the teenager feel more at ease. It must be recognised, however, that other family members may feel uncomfortable with such language.

Body image

Modern society is preoccupied with body image (Price, 2000) and adolescents are particularly concerned with how they appear in the eyes of others. Minor blemishes are considered a disaster to a healthy adolescent. The potential impact of altered appearance for those with serious illness is considerable (Fochtman, 1979).

It has been shown that, compared with a cohort of healthy adolescents, those with cancer portrayed very different concerns about their bodies (Chambas, 1991). The healthy teenagers were preoccupied with concerns that reflected the adolescent changes they were experiencing: acne, and size of breasts or penis ,whereas the teenagers with cancer were almost exclusively concerned about body image issues related to their disease or treatment. These included surgical scarring, hair loss, being stared at, and infertility.

Case study 7.3

Alex was a fifteen-year-old girl diagnosed with a primitive neuro-ectodermal tumour of her shoulder. She had received chemotherapy, radiotherapy and surgery during her initial treatment and two subsequent relapses. Alex had visible scarring around her neck from surgical excision and the insertion of a central venous line. Image was extremely important to Alex, even during palliation. She wore a wig to disguise her alopecia and was anxious to purchase a bikini that hid her central venous line for a family holiday. However, her greatest concern was the scarring around her shoulders and neckline and its impact on her appearance. She sought advice about camouflage make-up from a consultant at a local store, which made her feel able to 'show herself off' in public. She was also then able to attend a fashion shoot and had photographs taken in bridal wear and a glamorous off-the-shoulder gown.

The use of make-up to hide disfigurement or even pallor can help to maintain body image (McCarthy, 1995), although it may become increasingly difficult to disguise changes in appearance as disease progresses (Price, 2000).

The continuing importance of body image to adolescents, even when they are dying, is clearly illustrated in *Case study 7.3*. Relatively simple procedures involving the use of make-up can be highly effective and greatly improve self-esteem. Merely acknowledging with patients that body image is an issue can help. The willingness of professionals to explore potentially useful interventions will affirm that such issues are considered important.

Clothing is of great importance to young people and shopping for clothes a regular activity. Adolescents frequently engage in shopping expeditions with friends. However, for an adolescent whose physical condition is changed it can be demoralising. A teenager who is wheelchair-bound or incontinent and requiring nappies may find that clothes shopping is no longer a pleasurable experience, but one fraught with embarrassment and disappointment. Individual changing rooms may not be large enough to accommodate a wheelchair and communal rooms may be seen as unacceptable. Styles of clothing previously worn and/or considered cool and trendy may no longer be appropriate. Tight trousers may accentuate the bulk of a nappy, and hipsters or short skirts may be too revealing. Moreover, clothing may not hang correctly when the person is sitting in a wheelchair. The use of home shopping catalogues may circumvent some of the issues around trying on clothes in communal spaces and allow experimentation with different styles. Furthermore, it may be possible to reproduce some of the pleasure of peer group shopping through 'trying on' evenings.

Self-esteem

Level of self-esteem can profoundly affect an adolescent's development and ability to cope with the conflict and change that he/she is experiencing (Grant and Roberts, 1998). Threats to positive self-esteem pervade everyday life, through the media, in terms of what is considered acceptable physique, clothing, hair-style etc, and through the attitude of peer groups.

For the sick adolescent, however, there may be additional factors to consider. Merely being in the unfamiliar role of a patient, with its resultant dependence, can induce a loss of self-worth (Ritchie, 1992). The adolescent may even see him/herself as weak (Hinds *et al*, 1992). It is also clear that issues related to body image can impact negatively (Heiney, 1989). The effect of debilitating symptoms on self-image can be very damaging (Hinds *et al*, 1992); likewise, the physical changes of disease can result in low self-esteem (Tebbi *et al*, 1985).

Sexuality is particularly closely related to self-regard. Feeling able to evoke desire in another person results from positive feelings and beliefs about one's own personality and physical appearance (Grant and Roberts, 1998; Quinn, 2003). Accordingly, the physical changes of disease may make the adolescent feel that he/she is not sexually attractive (Tebbi *et al*, 1985).

Poor self-esteem may also result in social withdrawal (Lahteenmaki *et al*, 2002) and hence seclusion. This can compound the multiple existing threats to the sick adolescent's continued relations with his peer group.

Peer acceptance

The role of peer group increases in importance during adolescence (Thornes *et al*, 2001). Attitudes and opinions of peers are more important than those of adults, and acceptance by peers is important to an adolescent's self-worth (Fochtman, 1979; Grant and Roberts, 1998). Adolescents come to accept and like who they are through the support and acceptance of their peer group (Ellis, 1991). However, the pattern of normality for teenagers is very narrow and will not allow even minor dissimilarity, such as dress, music, accent (Swanick and Oliver, 1985). Adolescents exhibit clannish behaviour and intolerance of those who are different, resulting in exclusion (Erickson, 1968). The adolescent dying of cancer may be perceived as different and therefore become isolated from his/her peer group. Experience has shown, however, that when peers have been involved in the ongoing care of the sick adolescent, they are much more likely to continue to have an active role during palliation. This is, however, entirely dependent upon the wishes of the adolescent and their parents and peers.

Threats to peer support

As adolescence is normally one of the healthiest periods of a lifetime, the presence of symptoms is abnormal and will set the affected teenager apart from his peer group (Hinds *et al*, 1992). The severity of illness or symptoms can effectively restrict the teenager's social interactions, which may be reduced to encompass only family and health professionals (Nishimoto, 1995). Should diagnosis and treatment also have occurred during or shortly before the onset of adolescence, the likelihood of such diminished socialisation is increased.

Social isolation may also be 'driven' by the sick teenager himself, who may feel embarrassment with his peers regarding such issues as:

* reduced physical ability/impaired mobility, and hence the need for a wheelchair
* physical changes — scarring, emaciation or weight gain, moon face, nasogastric tube/central venous line
* the presence of symptoms — vomiting, seizures, drooling, squint, impaired speech.

Case study 7.4

R anjit was a thirteen-year-old boy with a brainstem glioma. He was very debilitated by his disease, which made him angry and frustrated. Ranjit had always been fiercely independent. He fought the need to use a wheelchair, but eventually found that he could not manage without it. However, he flatly refused to go anywhere in it if there was even the remotest chance that he would meet any of his friends from school. When asked about this, he said that he did not want any of them to see him 'like this'.

Case study 7.4 illustrates the impact of poor self-image on socialisation. It highlights Ranjit's feelings of dismay at the symptoms that were rendering him different from his peer group.

In adolescence, socialising with peers becomes more important than time spent with family. This transition can be a difficult time for parents and teenagers (Grant and Roberts, 1998). Nevertheless, when this process is interrupted by illness and the teenager becomes isolated it can be very painful for the family to observe. Conversely, it is possible to see how a family may not encourage, or even actively discourage, continued relations with those peers that they perceive as a bad influence.

Sexuality

Notwithstanding the lack of clearly identified milestones, other than puberty, it is evident that sexual development progresses throughout infancy and childhood (Gordon and Schroeder, 1995). Sexuality, however, arises as a central theme in teenage life (Heiney, 1989). It can be viewed as a by-product of the attempt to determine identity (Swanick and Oliver, 1985). Nevertheless, sexuality is pivotal in the development of the adolescent; this will include genital development, reproductive processes, social status, emotions and relationships (Chambas, 1991).

Adolescence is the time of sexual awakening for many young people (Thornes *et al,* 2001), with the emergence of hormone-related sex drive. Having cancer does not eradicate such sexual urges (Nishimoto, 1995). For a young person to be dying while experiencing these new feelings can be distressing. They may have to confront the knowledge that they may never kiss or become intimate with a partner. They are likely to grieve for their unfulfilled dreams, fuelled by magazines that they read and programmes they watch. Such thoughts and feelings may be difficult for the teenager to articulate and for the family to consider.

For some parents the notion of their child fulfilling his/her sexual desire may be distasteful. A wish to explore sexuality may not, however, be a desire to experience the act of intercourse. Sexuality can be expressed in a wide range of activities from which sexual pleasure is derived. These can include activities ranging from conversation, visual stimulation and masturbation through to intercourse (Heiney, 1989).

Case study 7.5

Craig was fifteen and receiving palliative care for leukaemia. Craig had been troubled with leg pain that had been difficult to control. He was also sleepy and inactive much of the time. His second cousin Mandy was seventeen, physically well developed and frequently wore revealing tops. The highlight of Craig's week were the visits from Mandy. Craig reported improved comfort and energy levels when she visited. His parents also noted that the more her breasts were on show the better Craig seemed to feel.

Case study 7.6

Sally was a fourteen-year-old with a metastatic bone tumour. During the palliative phase of her disease, Sally was generally low in mood and not communicating. She had, however, previously vocalised that she 'fancied' the two teenage sons of family friends. Sally had attended swimming club with the boys before her illness. During palliation, Sally would tolerate most interventions provided that they did not prohibit her from going to watch the boys at swimming club or spending the weekend at the caravan site, where the boys' parents also had a caravan.

Case studies 7.5 and *7.6* illustrate the adolescent's developing sexuality and, while neither teenager embarked upon a physical relationship, both were pursuing their sexual desires and thus deriving pleasure from their encounters.

Masturbation

Children masturbate and derive sexual pleasure from doing so from an early age (Gordon and Schroeder, 1995). As their physical appearance alters, adolescents become curious to explore these changes and through this will learn how to arouse themselves. This process forms the backdrop to later sexual encounters with chosen partners. In our modern culture, media coverage aimed at this age group supports their understanding; however, within society generally there seems to be reluctance coupled with embarrassment around masturbation and other such issues (Hooton, 1998). Those caring for adolescents must acknowledge that sexual expression through masturbation is normal, acceptable and common behaviour. Specific consideration should be given to the privacy of an adolescent being nursed in a semi-public place, eg. in the sitting room.

The sexually active teenager

Some young people will be sexually active (with or without their parents' knowledge) or have the desire to be so. Studies suggest that 30% of sixteen-year-olds have experienced intercourse before the legal age of consent (Ford *et al,* 1997). Indeed, it is not unusual for adolescents to engage in sexual intercourse at twelve to thirteen years of age (Graham, 1998).

For those young people already in an intimate relationship and with parental knowledge, continued sexual activity may be sustained. However, increasing frailty or disability can present concerns and practical problems. Likewise, symptoms or medication can also impact, eg. both anti-emetics and analgesia can lower sexual drive and affect sexual performance (Smith and Babaian, 1992). The teenager may desire to be touched and comforted in preference to having intercourse. The effect of such issues on a partner should not be underestimated. The partner may feel rejected or there may be a lack of understanding of the patient's wishes.

Some adolescents may view having intercourse as a way of affirming life (Heiney, 1989). The potential pressure on the partner of the dying teenager who wishes to experience foreplay, oral pleasure or sexual intercourse before dying may therefore be intense. These issues may lead the partner to end the relationship or to worry that the patient will end it. This fear may lead to consent to sexual intercourse without the desire to do so.

It is possible that within the enormity of the situation, the issue of contraception is overlooked or even avoided. The importance of continued use, or the initiation of, contraceptives should be highlighted by the professionals working with young people. It should not be presumed that having received treatment for cancer will mean that a partner is infertile. Moreover, the recent/current administration of agents such as oral etoposide, present a theoretical risk of foetal deformity (Bristol-Myers Pharmaceuticals, 2001).

Being the partner

Being the girlfriend or boyfriend of a dying adolescent can be demanding.

Case study 7.7

Jason was nineteen years old. His girlfriend Gemma, aged eighteen years, was dying of cancer. She lived with her parents. Gemma and Jason had been engaged for two years and one of Gemma's greatest wishes was to have a white wedding. This was organised in the last few months of her life. The arrangements for the wedding kept Gemma, Jason and Gemma's family very busy. Although Gemma was deteriorating physically, her determination to get married kept her going. Gemma and Jason's wedding was a great success. They had a brief honeymoon in Blackpool and returned to live at Gemma's parents' house. Gemma died three months later and Jason returned to his parent's house.

In *Case study 7.7*, Jason was already a widower at nineteen years of age. He will have experienced a multitude of emotions during Gemma's illness and will have had to deal with the fact that he would lose her. The responsibilities and knowledge that a partner will soon die is immense at any age, but may be particularly difficult within this age group, who still have the majority of their life ahead of them. Future relationships may be coloured by the experience. There may be a reluctance to engage in other intimate relationships to protect themselves or out of respect for, or memory of, the dead partner. However, the focus of attention and support may remain with the parents, and the emotional needs of the partner can become minimised. Furthermore, the adolescent's peer group may find it difficult to provide support in a situation that is outside their knowledge base. It is vital, therefore, that provision is made to support the young partner during and in the aftermath of his/her bereavement; it may be difficult, however, to get the bereaved adolescent partner to utilise this support.

Risk-taking behaviour

The drive to explore life and develop identity through risk taking is part of the adolescent developmental process, and therefore common to all young people, sick or well. The adolescent with cancer will potentially confront the same issues regarding smoking, drugs, alcohol and sex as healthy teenagers (Barr,

2001). It has been shown that smoking and alcohol consumption is as prevalent among adolescent survivors of cancer as in healthy adolescents (Hollen and Hobbie, 1996; Michelagnoli and Viner, 2001). Furthermore, as with sexual intercourse (Heiney, 1989), risk taking may be viewed as life affirming by dying teenagers. Equally, they may feel that they have nothing to lose in pursuit of such behaviours.

Talking to adolescents

Adolescence is notably a period of limited communication. Many parents can recount stories of the brief grunting responses of their teenagers. When caring for a dying teenager the challenge is to find a balance between respecting the young person's privacy and showing availability and willingness to talk. Adolescents need the opportunity to be able to voice their feelings (Hollis and Morgan, 2001). It is, however, known that parents often assume an executive role during treatment, whereby they manage how and what is discussed with young people about their illness (Young *et al*, 2003). Such communication patterns may also prevail in the palliative phase of disease. While working in partnership with parents, professionals should encourage honesty and endeavour to foster a conducive relationship, in order to enable adolescents to discuss their condition and vocalise concerns.

Equally, when attempting to talk to a teenager about his/her impending death, individual coping mechanisms should be respected (Fochtman, 1979). Denial is frequently employed as a coping strategy by adolescents (Ritchie, 1992). Despite being aware of the palliative nature of their disease, many teenagers are reported as having a positive outlook for the future (Zeltzer *et al*, 1980). When denial and other coping strategies fail, hostility, projection of anger and depression can ensue (Rechner, 1990).

Spirituality

For a few young people, spiritual needs are fully met through their religious convictions; for many adolescents, however, organised religion is alien. Nevertheless, spiritual concerns are universal (Highfield, 1992), and for an adolescent facing untimely death, spiritual concerns may dominate over physical needs.

During health, adolescents often express their spirituality in their actions. They may demonstrate their beliefs through the unerring pursuit of such issues as vegetarianism, expressions of disgust at life's injustices, or a demonstration of their identity through a dogged adherence to a particular style. When life is threatened by illness, some adolescents will cling determinedly to the ideals and beliefs that they pursued in health, often with a greater sense of urgency. However, for many at this time there will also be a strong spiritual need to find a sense of purpose and fulfilment in the life that they have led and a way to ensure that their memory and actions will, in some way, live on.

In an attempt to reassure their child, parents may make unrealistic promises about getting well or not suffering, or even give an assurance that there is an afterlife. Adolescents may feel unable to express their own uncertainties to their parents. Some will, however, find that they are able to share their doubts and thoughts more readily with others (illustrated in *Case study 7.8*).

Meeting a person's spiritual needs means accepting their range of beliefs, doubts, fears and anxieties as valid expressions of where and who they are, and affirming them with no preconditions of our own (Penson and Fisher, 1991). In *Case study 7.8*, a member of the extended family became the adolescent's confidante; likewise, a friend, sibling or even a professional may find themselves in this role.

Case study 7.8

Rhiannon, aged thirteen, knew that she had another tumour in her lungs but had been told that the new oral chemotherapy she was on would probably get rid of it. As Rhiannon became weaker, her parents reassured her that her weakness was just a part of the process of getting well again, 'Don't you remember how sick the chemo made you the first time before you got better?' Rhiannon did not contradict her parents, but did ask to see her Aunt Christine more often.

When Rhiannon talked about being worried, Christine did not just try to reassure her but asked what she was worried about. She would sit and hold Rhiannon's hand as she shouted how unfair it was that she was always too ill to do the things she'd love to do, and listened as Rhiannon talked disjointedly about the past and future. Together they made an album of 'Rhiannon's Favourite Photos'. Christine told her that the day Rhiannon had been born was the happiest day ever and that she would always remember it. The highlight of the album was the photo of Rhiannon receiving a medal for modern dancing at the local theatre. Rhiannon told Christine that she thought that Eric, her two-year-old brother, might like to see the album when he was older.

Rhiannon talked too about her belief that her late grandma was her guardian angel and how she would always look out for Rhiannon whatever happened. Rhiannon wondered openly whether aunt Christine would be a sort of guardian angel to her mum on earth. Christine promised that she would always try to look after Rhiannon's mum.

The role of the professional

For professionals working within the paediatric arena, the importance of the ability to move freely between the attitude, care and language that is required for differing age groups is paramount. The methods and terminology used with a young child may be patronising to an adolescent.

Clearly, adolescents have different needs from other paediatric patients, and those with cancer have specific requirements. Adolescents need stability when their future is in doubt (Hollis and Morgan, 2001). The value of continuity of staff is therefore immeasurable, and the mutual trust and respect developed early in the disease process invaluable (Fochtman, 1979).

Professionals caring for teenagers with cancer should identify the obstacles to their pursuit of independence. It has been recognised that encouraging control, responsibility and involvement in decision making around disease and treatment issues is beneficial (Barr, 2001; Hollis and Morgan, 2001). These guidelines continue to be appropriate and of great importance in the palliative phase of disease.

The concept of hope is also recognised as being vitally important to adolescents (Hinds, 1988; Hinds and Martin, 1988). Professionals need to find strategies to foster hope in order to help the teenager find his own coping strategies.

Summary

Adolescence is a period of enormous upheaval, both emotionally and physically. Facing imminent death in this time period is especially challenging. Both parents and professional carers will need to consider their unique needs and endeavour to respond appropriately.

References

Barr RD (2001) The adolescent with cancer. *Eur J Cancer* **37**(12): 1523–30
Bristol-Myers Pharmaceuticals (2001) Specific product characteristics of VePesid. Capsules. Accessed from medical.information@bms.com on 31.10.02
Chambas K (1991) Sexual concerns of adolescents with cancer. *J Pediatr Oncol Nurs* **8**(4): 165–72

Copeland DR (1998) Rehabilitation of an adolescent with medulloblastoma. *Cancer Pract* **6**(3): 138–42

Ellis JA (1991) Coping with adolescent cancer: its a matter of adaptation. *J Pediatr Oncol Nurs* **8**(1): 10–17

Enskar K, Carlsson M, Golsater M, Hamrin E (1997) Symptom distress and life situation in adolescents with cancer. *Cancer Nurs* **20**(1): 23–33

Erickson EH (1968) *Identity: Youth and Crisis.* 1983 reissue. Faber and Faber, London

Fochtman D (1979) How adolescents live with leukemia. *Cancer Nurs* **2**(1): 27–31

Ford N, Halliday J, Little J (1997) Changes in drug use and sexual lifestyles of young people in Somerset, 1990-1996. Survey commisioned by Somerset Health Authority. Department of Geography, University of Exeter

Gordon BN, Schroeder CS (1995) Normal sexual development. In: *Sexuality: A developmental approach to problems.* Plenum Press, New York and London: 1–21

Graham G (1998) Promoting young people's sexual health. In: Harrison T (Ed). *Children and Sexuality.* Baillière Tindall, London: 162–99

Grant JM, Roberts J (1998) Psychological development: sex and sexuality in adolescence. In: Harrison T (Ed). *Children and Sexuality.* Baillière Tindall, London: 67–87

Heiney SP (1989) Adolescents with cancer: sexual and reproductive issues. *Cancer Nurs* **12**(2): 95–101

Heiney SP, Wells LM, Coleman B *et al* (1990) Lasting impressions: a psychosocial support programme for adolescents with cancer and their parents. *Cancer Nurs* **13**(1): 3–20

Highfield MF (1992) Spiritual health of oncology patients: nurse and patient. *Cancer Nurs* **15**(1): 1–8

Hinds P (1988) Adolescent hopefulness in illness and health. *ANS Adv Nurs Sci* **10**: 79–88

Hinds P, Martin J (1988) Hopefulness: the self-sustaining process in adolescents with cancer. *Nurs Res* **37**: 336–40

Hinds PS, Quargnenti AG, Wentz TJ (1992) Measuring symptom distress in adolescents with cancer. *J Pediatr Oncol Nurs* **9**(2): 84–6

Hollen PJ, Hobbie WI (1996) Decision-making and risk behaviours of cancer-surviving adolescents and their peers. *J Pediatr Oncol Nurs* **13**: 121–34

Hollis R, Morgan S (2001) The adolescent with cancer — at the edge of no-man's land. *Lancet Oncol* **2**(1): 43–8

Hooton S (1998) Contemporary cultural influences upon the development of sexuality, sexual expression and mortality of children living in the UK. In: Harrison T (Ed). *Children and Sexuality.* Baillière Tindall, London: 19–41

Lahteenmaki PM *et al* (2002) Childhood cancer patients at school. *Eur J Cancer* **38**: 1227–40

McCarthy D (1995) Palliative care in adolescence. *Eur J Palliat Care* **2**(2): 52–4

Michelagnoli M, Viner R (2001) Commentary. *Eur J Cancer* **37**: 1527–30

Nishimoto PW (1995) Sex and sexuality in the cancer patient. *Nurse Pract Forum* **6**(4): 221–7

Penson J, Fisher R (1991) *Palliative Care for People with Cancer*. Edward Arnold, London

Pinkerton CR, Cushing P, Sepion B (1994) *Childhood Cancer Management. A practical handbook*. Chapman and Hall, London

Price B (2000) Altered body image: managing social encounters. *Int J Palliat Nurs* **6**(4): 179–85

Quinn B (2003) Sexual health in cancer care. *Nurs Times* **99**(4): 32–4

Reres M (1980) Stressors on adolescents. *Family Community Medicine* **2**: 31–41

Rechner M (1990) Adolescents with cancer: getting on with life. *J Pediatr Oncol Nurs* **7**: 139–44

Ritchie MA (1992) Psychosocial functioning of adolescents with cancer: a developmental perspective. *Oncol Nurs Forum* **19**(10): 1497–501

Roberts CS, Turney ME, Knowles AM (1998) Psychosocial issues of adolescents with cancer. *Soc Work Health Care* **27**(4): 3–18

Smith DB, Babaian RJ (1992) The effects of treatment for cancer on male fertility and sexuality. *Cancer Nurs* **15**(4): 271–5

Swanick M, Oliver RW (1985) Psychological adjustment in adolescence. *Nursing* **40**: 1179–81

Tebbi C, Stern M, Boyle M *et al* (1985) The role of social support systems in adolescent cancer amputees. *Cancer* **56**: 965–71

Thornes R, on behalf of the Joint Working Party on Palliative Care for Adolescents and Young Adults (2001) *Palliative Care for Young People Aged 13–24*. Edited by Elston S. Association for Children with Life-threatening or Terminal Conditions and their Families, Bristol; National Council for Hospice and Specialist Palliative Care Services, London; and Scottish Partnership Agency for Palliative and Cancer Care, Edinburgh

Weekes DP, Kagan SH (1994) Adolescents completing cancer therapy: meaning, perception and coping. *Oncol Nurs Forum* **21**(4): 663–70

Young B, Dixon-Woods M, Windridge KC, Heney D (2003) Managing communication with young people who have a potentially life-threatening chronic illness: qualitative study of patients and parents. *Br Med J* **326**: 305–8

Zeltzer L, Kellerman J, Ellenberg L *et al* (1980) Psychologic effects of illness in adolescents. II. Impact of illness in adolescents — crucial issues and coping styles. *J Pediatr* **97**: 132–8

8

It's a good job, but it's stressful

Caring for patients is inherently demanding – nursing is recognised to be one of the most stressed professional groups in the UK (Crouch, 2003). Surveys have continually shown that up to a third of NHS nurses experience mental health problems, most commonly anxiety and depression (Borrell, 1996). Furthermore, within the paediatric arena, these demands are amplified by the need to connect not only with the child, but also the parents, siblings and extended family (Spinetta *et al*, 2000; Barnes, 2001).

Working within paediatric palliative care is considered a rewarding career option. However, this environment can be particularly stressful (Barnes, 2001). Nurses working in this discipline frequently encounter frightened, distressed and vulnerable families. Their role regularly requires them to cope with the demands of terminal care, advocacy, symptom control, and physical and psychosocial care. For nurses new to this discipline, the responsibilities might appear overwhelming: 'How can I make a difference?' 'How can I cope?' Many personal accounts suggest that palliative care nurses do not always cope, with young or inexperienced staff being particularly vulnerable to stress (Vachon, 1998).

Traditionally, nurses learn to adopt coping strategies in difficult professional situations through trial and error. For many this approach has been successful; for others it has not, resulting in stress, burnout and, in some cases, the decision to leave the profession (Spinetta *et al*, 2000). Written and formally taught guidance on appropriate coping strategies and role boundaries has often been limited. Relying on nurses to approach, manage and survive difficult encounters with limited support is not ideal, leaving both the nurse and the family vulnerable.

With more than ten years' experience in paediatric palliative care, the West Midlands Paediatric Macmillan Team (WMPMT) has encountered a range of complex professional issues while caring for dying children and their families. The team is therefore in a good position to offer some approaches to practice-based problems that have been successful.

This chapter draws on evidence from the literature and the team's experiences to highlight key areas where the recognition of potential dilemmas may help others to develop strategies to reduce stress levels and improve practice. The chapter is specifically targeted at nurses new to paediatric palliative care, although more experienced practitioners may find the content thought provoking. Problems that may confront nurses will be explored through a series of clinical vignettes based on case studies, entitled:

⌘ Thinking about death and dying.
⌘ Unrealistic expectations.
⌘ Over-involvement.
⌘ Bereavement support.

It is acknowledged that the structure, roles and responsibilities of individual teams may differ from those of this team. The fundamental issues, however, will be similar.

Thinking about death and dying

As children, both our parents and the immediate environment shape our experiences of ourselves and the world around us. As we mature, teachers, friends and the media begin to influence our attitudes and understanding of who and what we are. We acquire what have been described as internal models — 'a framework for meaning' — which we draw on to validate and make sense of new situations and experiences (Riches and Dawson, 2000).

It has been suggested that, in the modern world, these internal models fail to equip individuals with the ability to make sense of childhood death (Riches and Dawson, 2000). The cultural norm assumes that people die when they grow old. The concept of death and dying is largely left unspoken. Lack of experience, therefore, may mean that individuals have limited abilities to create personal philosophies and belief systems that can accommodate the acceptance of childhood death, particularly if the individual exists outside a religious community.

Clearly, then, the death of a child or children may compromise an individual's belief systems and leave him/her struggling to adjust in an unfamiliar emotional arena. *Case study 8.1* highlights an example of this within the paediatric oncology setting.

In this extreme example, it is clear that Kirandeep's death led Sandra to contemplate the potential of her own death and the death of those closest to her. In the following weeks, Sandra was clearly struggling to make sense of what had happened.

Case study 8.1

Sandra was the named nurse for Kirandeep, aged four years. Kirandeep died unexpectedly during bone marrow transplant. Sandra was so distressed that she was unable to care for Kirandeep's body and her family during the rest of her shift. Kirandeep's family were concerned for Sandra's wellbeing. Sandra was tearful and distracted in the following weeks. She took sick leave. On her return to work, it transpired that Sandra had never seen a dead child's body before. Subsequently, she suffered repeated nightmares about the possibility of her own children dying and became fixated with the thought that she too may die prematurely. Ward nurses were worried that they should have somehow known that Sandra had not seen a dead child's body before. They felt they had 'let her down'.

Within the paediatric oncology setting, exposure to death and dying are commonplace. It is therefore essential for nurses working in the specialty to reflect upon feelings about their own mortality and examine their own belief systems (Gill, 1995; McSherry, 1996). The nurse's ability to help others explore and face impending death will otherwise be seriously compromised. It is unacceptable that Kirandeep's family were confronted with Sandra's difficulties at a time when the focus of attention should have been themselves and their daughter.

Staff new to the discipline should be encouraged to explore their beliefs and personal resources for coping with these challenges:

⌘ What is their previous experience of death?
⌘ What coping methods have they used previously and how successful have they been?
⌘ What sources of both professional and personal support can they identify?

Discussion should not, however, be limited to those joining the unit. The need for self-awareness and the nurturing of coping strategies must be encouraged and ongoing. This should be facilitated by the unit through staff development programmes and an environment that encourages personal and team reflection (Harding, 1996; Spinetta *et al*, 2000).

Feedback from nursing staff on the oncology unit at Birmingham Children's Hospital has demonstrated that they particularly value the opportunity to participate in debriefing sessions after inpatient deaths. These can take several forms:

⌘ Allocated time in handover meetings. This can, however, prove problematic if the ward is particularly busy.
⌘ Formal sessions facilitated by an in-house bereavement officer or alternative facilitator. These are usually most effective if they are organised soon after the death.

⌘ One-to-one sessions with an appropriate individual, such as a Macmillan nurse, Sargent social worker or senior ward nurse.

The style of debriefing will vary, depending on personal and team need. Moreover, individual nurses may not require these meetings after every death. What is important, is that nurses are aware of the availability and appropriateness of such sessions within the unit. Similarly, community nurses will often benefit from the opportunity to talk through events around a child's death.

Perhaps if Sandra in *Case study 8.1* had previously been encouraged to share her inexperience of death or reflect on her own belief systems, she might have coped better. A policy of mentoring new staff and providing access to clinical supervision would act as a further safeguard to monitor previously unrecognised and extreme responses to caring for dying children.

Nurses also have a responsibility to develop ways of caring for themselves (McAliley *et al*, 1996; Barnes, 2001). Outside interests that distract from the workplace including physical exercise, hobbies and an active social life have all been reported as positive coping strategies (Spinetta *et al*, 2000; Hicks and Lavender, 2001). Nurses must also be aware of personal trigger factors that exacerbate stress (Hicks and Lavender, 2001). For example, a nurse may feel overwhelming distress when caring for a dying child who is of a similar age to her own child. In these circumstances, it is reasonable to request not to be directly involved in the care of that child where possible.

There is no single strategy that will enable all nurses to cope with the stress of caring for dying children and their families. The key to a successful coping strategy does appear to be the ability of the individual to create a philosophy of life that accommodates death. This can, however, be supported in the workplace by an environment that encourages both self-awareness and reflection.

KEY POINTS

◆ Nurses have a responsibility to develop ways of caring for themselves and of creating coping strategies.

◆ Nurses working in paediatric palliative care must acknowledge their own mortality and reflect on their individual belief systems.

◆ The work environment should facilitate reflection on different philosophies and experiences of death.

◆ Staff development programmes, clinical supervision and team discussions should enhance this reflection.

Unrealistic expectations

The literature suggests that palliative care nurses may have unrealistic expectations of what they are able to achieve (Vachon, 1998). Nurses cite the inability to provide good symptom control as exacerbating stress in their jobs. Anything other than a truly symptom-free death has been considered to be failure, leaving nurses with feelings of regret and inadequacy when symptoms are unresolved. These feelings may be magnified within the paediatric arena (Spinetta *et al*, 2000; Barnes, 2001).

There is also a common misconception that having access to specialist palliative care support services will ensure that a patient will be free from adverse symptoms and avoid a traumatic death. No individual, team or organisation, however, can fully control illness and death (Vachon, 1998): children will occasionally die with unresolved and perhaps distressing side-effects of their disease process. *Case study 8.2* explores these issues within a paediatric oncology setting.

Case study 8.2

Julie had recently joined the paediatric Macmillan team. Leroy, aged thirteen, had been receiving treatment for a brainstem tumour. He was now having palliative care at home and was in the terminal phase of his disease. When mum asked Julie how he would die, Julie said he would become increasingly tired and would eventually fall into a coma. Julie explained that the Macmillan team would be able to deal with any symptoms that Leroy might experience. Leroy did, however, suffer with persistent vomiting during treatment. This continued into palliative care and was never resolved. Leroy also experienced seizures; despite attempts to control these, they were a feature of his last weeks of life. When Leroy died, Julie reflected on his death. She felt responsible for his poor symptom control and believed that she had failed in her role.

This case study is a good example of how nurses may have unrealistic expectations of what they are able to achieve in palliative care. The implications can be far-reaching:

* Leroy's family may feel cheated. Julie failed to explain that some symptoms can persist during palliative care.
* Julie may be apprehensive about future contact with Leroy's family.
* Julie may experience anxiety when faced with another palliative care patient.
* Julie may lose confidence in her competence as a nurse in future decision-making.

In an attempt to comfort the family of a dying child, it is easy to make sweeping statements that later prove untrue. Platitudes such as 'We'll keep him pain free' or 'He will drift into a coma' are often unfounded and prove to be incorrect. From the outset of palliation, both families and nursing staff need to be clear about what can be achieved. Although it is possible for the majority of children to die with their symptoms well controlled (see *Chapter 5*), experience teaches nurses not to make broad generalisations. Statements suggesting that symptoms can be minimised are more appropriate. It was also misguided of Julie to suggest that Leroy would die in a certain way. It is better to look back on previous deaths, giving examples of possible events around death without being prescriptive.

Julie has also judged the success of palliative care solely on the basis of alleviation of symptoms. This does not take account of the holistic nature of palliative care and may therefore negate months of skilled interventions supporting the child and family. By being more realistic with families, nurses will give them more accurate expectations of symptom control. Palliative care teams should take the time to discuss patients on a regular basis (see *Chapter 3*). These meetings should allow nurses the opportunity to explore their own feelings and limitations within a supportive environment. By utilising the skills of more experienced staff it may be possible to explore palliation in more detail. In this situation, alternative approaches to patient management could have been debated, and time given to rebuilding Julie's confidence and self-esteem.

Equally unrealistic is the perception that palliative care teams should have the ability to resolve discordance within family units. Some families will present at diagnosis with complex emotional dynamics and perhaps years of ill-feeling between various family members. In an ideal world, the diagnosis of a life-threatening illness would unite individuals and past differences would be forgotten. The reality, however, is different. It is not uncommon for families to continue to feud during the palliative phase of a child's disease. The palliative care team's responsibility lies primarily with the wellbeing of the child and immediate family. Advice on shielding the sick child from disagreements may well be the best that can be achieved.

There are times when other issues within the family remain unresolved. For example, a dying adolescent may be anxious to speak to family members about his imminent death, but no relatives feel emotionally equipped to have that conversation, so the young person dies missing the opportunity to express his thoughts and feelings directly to them. Individual team members can blame themselves for what they perceive as their inability to enable these conversations to take place. Communicating with and advocating for families is extremely challenging (see *Chapter 4*). However frustrating and upsetting these circumstances might be, they are not uncommon. They do not, however, represent the failure of any one practitioner. Rather, they are the consequence of working with unique family units whose members have diverse and often conflicting needs and equally conflicting coping strategies.

Finally, it is vital that no single individual should have the sole responsibility for orchestrating a child's symptom control and palliative care. Co-working palliative care within the multiprofessional team will ensure that feelings of personal responsibility or failure are kept to a minimum, and that support for all team members is maximised.

KEY POINTS

◆ Sometimes children die with symptoms that are unresolved.

◆ Some deaths are traumatic. This does not necessarily represent failure.

◆ Family dynamics are complex. Often psychosocial issues remain unresolved.

◆ Palliative care nurses should co-work cases within a team environment.

Over-involvement

The concept of the over-involved relationship has been reported extensively in the literature (Morse, 1991; Aranda, 2001; Williams, 2001). It is increasingly being identified in the paediatric arena and has been recognised as an important source of stress in paediatric oncology nursing (Harding, 1996). Morse (1991) describes over-involvement as the development of an intimate relationship between the nurse and the patient.

At the outset, the relationship may appear to be no different from any other. Subtle changes in behaviour patterns may, however, develop, becoming exaggerated with time. The nurse may become territorial about care giving, inappropriately disclosing aspects of her personal life, spending increasing periods of time attending to the family's needs and fostering a 'special relationship' (Rushton *et al*, 1996; Hicks and Lavender, 2001). This may appear to be the embodiment of patient advocacy, as the patient's wishes are paramount. As individuals, however, and within a wider team, nurses have a commitment to other patients, colleagues and the institution. As Morse (1991) indicated in her study, these considerations are often marginalised by the over-involved nurse. *Case study 8.3* will be used to explore some of the negative consequences of over-involvement.

Case study 8.3

Mary is a paediatric community nurse. She had been caring for Chloe, aged eight, for several years during her leukaemia treatment. Chloe progressed, requiring palliative care, and was at home. Mary undertook the majority of the care giving on her own. She was reluctant to joint visit with colleagues or let others visit in her place. She felt that she had a special relationship with Mary's mother Lisa. Lisa, a single parent, asked Mary to be with her when Chloe died. Mary agreed.

This case study provides an example of over-involvement. There are many likely consequences of Mary's actions:

⌘ Mary is excluding her colleagues from care giving — this may cause tension in the team.
⌘ Mary will not be able to assess or deliver care effectively in isolation.
⌘ Without prior contact with other team members, Lisa may be reluctant to refer to anyone other than Mary.
⌘ Mary will be unable to predict when Chloe will die; she may ultimately have to stay with or close to the family for several days or weeks to ensure that she is there when Chloe dies, to the detriment of her other patients.
⌘ Mary may be physically and mentally exhausted by the time Chloe dies.

It is clear that Mary is not adopting a team approach to care. As no single individual can provide optimum care in isolation, Mary is trying to provide an unsustainable service. Lisa and Chloe would benefit from the input of the wider team, who could offer support and alternative ideas on symptom control. Few teams would be able to sustain this level of input indefinitely, let alone an individual.

Why is Mary nurturing this dependency? Is it naivety or a result of personal needs not met elsewhere (Rushton *et al*, 1996)? Some might say that her commitment is commendable. If she is able to be there when Chloe dies, Lisa will be grateful; if not, Lisa may feel betrayed. Conversely, Mary may be accused of exploiting Lisa's vulnerability. A family of a child with any illness is vulnerable (Totya, 1996; Hicks and Lavender, 2001). The situation is further exacerbated when they are faced with their child's impending death. The overwhelming emotions and loss of control compel parents to look to nurses for guidance. Nurses such as Mary should recognise that, while families remain vulnerable, they themselves are in the privileged position of being trusted to act in the family's best interest. They must use this trust appropriately – working with the family to create a relationship and service that is professionally credible. Mary has failed to do this. Furthermore, she may fail other families. Confronted with two or three palliative patients at any one time, it is unlikely that Mary will be able to offer the same level of input. The strain of providing 'special' care to families may also take its toll, as over-involved relationships have been reported as contributing to increasing stress and burnout (Vachon, 1998).

Ideally, Mary would be functioning within a team that would recognise and address this behaviour from the outset. The over-involved relationship rarely starts out that way. It's insidious onset makes it difficult to detect for the nurse, the family and the wider team. The most reliable way of safeguarding against over-involvement is to ensure that teams operate within recognised boundaries (*Table 8.1*).

Table 8.1: Why have boundaries?
⌘ Without boundaries, relationships are ill defined and open to misinterpretation
⌘ Boundaries safeguard against abuses and prevent ambiguity
⌘ Boundaries are set in order to limit the intervention by the nurse to that which is in the best interests of the patient
Rushton *et al* (1996)

Boundaries should be based upon guidance from professional regulating bodies (Nursing and Midwifery Council, 2002), while also reflecting the policies of local service providers. Ultimately, they should represent guidelines on what is considered acceptable, professional and credible practice.

With appropriate boundaries in place, Mary's team would question their exclusion from Chloe's care almost from the outset. Mary would be encouraged to consider her actions and assess their positive and negative implications. Without documented boundaries, however, the team may feel unable to challenge her. An inexperienced team may even fail to recognise her actions as over-involved and commend her commitment to care.

Examples of boundaries within the WMPMT

The team is committed to:

⌘ Working in accordance with their job description and operational policy.
⌘ Keeping personal lives separate from professional responsibilities.
⌘ Not giving home telephone numbers and addresses to families.
⌘ Not allowing work to impinge on off-duty and annual leave.
⌘ Recognising that no individual nurse is indispensable.
⌘ Ensuring that families are provided with a team approach to care.
⌘ Ensuring that all families have access to an equitable service.

Although these statements are realistic, seeing them in print could, for some, potentially evoke images of a sterile, uncaring team. This is not the case. The results of audit from families and professional groups show that families in the care of the WMPMT feel 'special' and well supported. Moreover, boundaries are not designed to prevent nurses from 'caring'. Boundaries help to clarify the nature of the nurse–family relationship, allowing the nurse to demonstrate real concern for the welfare of the child and family, while safeguarding the best interests of families and the wellbeing of the nurse.

Appropriate boundaries will vary, depending on the remit of particular teams and individuals. They may also be flexible in special circumstances. In teams where clear boundaries are not yet established, it may be invaluable to have input from a skilled external facilitator to lead the necessary discussions, especially where there is discrepancy in the views of team members. Boundaries, however, are difficult to monitor, and require individuals and teams to adopt a sensitive, open-door approach to their discussion. Those who stray outside these boundaries need support to adjust their relationships and interventions (Totya, 1996). The basic premise, however, remains the same: there has to be a beginning and an end to what nurses expect and are expected to do. Failure to recognise this leaves both nurses and families vulnerable to over-involvement.

KEY POINTS

◆ It is easy to become over-involved with patients and families in the paediatric oncology setting.

◆ Over-involvement is characterised by the fostering of special relationships with families, being territorial about care giving, inappropriate self-disclosure, and out-of-hours socialising.

◆ Over-involvement represents behaviour considered unacceptable by professional regulating bodies and the institution.

◆ It is essential for paediatric palliative care teams to have guidelines that set out the boundaries of their professional responsibilities when caring for families.

Bereavement support

Case study 8.4

Barbara is a paediatric Macmillan nurse. She had previously nursed David aged four, who died three years ago. Since then she had been visiting Steve and Tanya, his parents, offering bereavement support. They lived ninety minutes away from her base and she had been seeing them on average every two months. The visit normally took up most of the day. Barbara had struggled to disengage from this family. They tell Barbara that they enjoyed her visits and asked her to be godparent to their new baby daughter.

Case study 8.4 (below) explores the complexities of bereavement support. As in previous scenarios, the erosion of boundaries has become problematic. This case study is a good example of bereavement support that has become problematic. Although Barbara is looking to withdraw from the relationship, Steve and Tanya are hoping to formalise her inclusion within the family unit.

⌘ Barbara needs to begin to reduce her visits: the team cannot sustain this level of contact.

⌘ Steve and Tanya will be hurt: they enjoy her visits.

⌘ The family's request for Barbara to become a godmother needs careful handling.

Within the paediatric oncology setting, staff within both the unit and community teams may know children and their families for many years. These ongoing, often intense relationships may result in staff being referred to as almost 'one of the family' (Hicks and Lavender, 2001). With the death of their child, families can often feel the need to hold on to these close relationships for some time.

Clearly, what is missing in Barbara's bereavement support is structure and direction. Steve and Tanya have been misled or misinterpreted the nature of their relationship with Barbara. They cannot fail to be upset when they realise she intends to reduce her input. After all, she appears to have become increasingly like a member of the family. Perhaps Barbara was unaware of how important to them she has now become. Conversely, the family may have unwittingly contributed to her inability to withdraw. Statements such as 'We feel so much better when you've been' or 'You're our favourite nurse' are positive and rewarding (Hicks and Lavender, 2001). Every nurse appreciates positive reinforcement with regard to the standard of their care giving. It is clear that Steve and Tanya valued Barbara's input. These compliments can, however, be seductive. For some nurses, they may even bring about unnecessary visits to support personal needs.

Furthermore, if Barbara has sustained contact with Steve and Tanya because she believes they are experiencing pathological grief, she is misguided in her actions. Barbara is unlikely to be a trained bereavement counsellor and should therefore have referred the family to more specialist services.

Whatever the motivation, Barbara now needs to disengage, recognising that her workload can no longer sustain these meetings. In order to minimise the family's distress, she should discuss appropriate strategies with the wider team and management.

In recognition of the potential for similar dilemmas, the WMPMT adhere to a two-year bereavement protocol (see *Appendix 4*). This recommends a framework for contact that is both flexible and supportive. Families are told of the time frame: if, after two years, they feel they need further input, this can be negotiated. Otherwise, only they initiate any future contact. The protocol also reduces uncertainty among staff as to when and for how long families should be contacted.

The request for Barbara to become a godmother will need to be discussed with both the team and management at length. Questions regarding the potential enormity of the commitment will need to be explored. Barbara needs to explore her own and the family's expectations of the role of godmother. She also needs to consider seriously whether she is prepared to be allied to this family for life, and whether, if asked, she could make such a commitment to other families. If Barbara decides to say no to this family, she may find it helpful to refer to the team's boundaries and/or policies in explaining her decision to them. Helping the family to understand that for her to become the child's godmother would breach professional guidelines may help them to understand her dilemma while recognising the honour of being asked to take on the role.

Having reflected on the advantages and disadvantages, it is ultimately down to each individual to make a choice. Teams can, however, guide the decision-making.

Within the case studies, several themes emerge as strategies for managing challenging situations: teamwork, communication and supervision.

KEY POINTS

◆ Bereavement support should be structured.

◆ Nurses should discuss this structure with families.

◆ Nurses should be mindful of the need to disengage from families.

◆ Nurses caseloads can rarely accommodate prolonged bereavement support.

◆ Nurses need to be aware of other agencies that may be able to provide more specialist/prolonged support to bereaved families.

Teamwork

This chapter repeatedly advocates the need to adopt a team approach to care. Being part of a collaborative, competent and supportive team is professionally rewarding and makes work pleasurable (Vachon, 1998). Having team philosophies, goals and boundaries also gives individuals more control over the care they deliver (Barnes, 2001).

Teams need to check that they are functioning as a unit. It is possible to give the impression of a cohesive service when in reality there is, for example, a team of three, with three entirely different approaches to care. Mentoring of less experienced staff should promote consistency in practice (Hicks and Lavender, 2001). Teams need to meet regularly and be respectful of the individuality of their members. Experience has shown that team-building exercises with outside facilitators are beneficial.

Some nurses may find themselves as individual practitioners within a unit, eg. the only outreach nurse. It is advisable that they align themselves to experienced ward staff and other members of the multiprofessional team, creating a forum for support and some system for cover during time off. It is not possible to deliver effective paediatric palliative care in isolation.

Communication

The existence of a team and team meetings are meaningless if nurses' opinions, knowledge base and skills are not shared within them. Dilemmas need discussion. Team members should feel able to contribute, and confident that their suggestions will be valued. It is easy to talk about successful interactions with families, but much harder to talk about perceived failures.

Aspects of each of this chapter's case studies have previously been issues for the team. Sharing these experiences has contributed to the professional development of individual nurses and helped to shape the philosophies of the wider team. These philosophies have changed considerably since the team's inception. Talking about sensitive issues can be challenging, and meetings therefore need to be receptive and non-judgmental. Failure to facilitate such a forum can create a culture where anxieties are kept concealed, issues are unresolved and potentially problematic relationships go 'underground' (Aranda, 2001).

Supervision

This chapter has frequently discussed the benefits of peer supervision. Paediatric palliative care nurses should, however, also seek clinical supervision from outside the team. This is an alternative forum where nurses' competence and confidence can be developed. A skilled supervisor need not have specific knowledge of the discipline; his/her experiences will, however, facilitate reflection and professional growth. Each individual nurse has a responsibility to acquire a suitable supervisor. The team have utilised supervisors from a variety of settings such as social workers, counsellors and adult palliative care services. Their inclusion within the team's support strategy has proved invaluable.

Summary

Through the case studies, the WMPMT has shared some of the problems encountered since its inception over ten years ago. The team has at times felt stressed and disillusioned in its work, and interventions have sometimes been misguided and problematic. The majority, however, have been professional, competent and rewarding. Audit of our practice confirms this. We have used these experiences — both positive and negative — to re-evaluate and redefine our practice. Sharing these experiences by means of the case studies may enable others to avoid potential pitfalls. Individuals may not wholly agree with our philosophies, but this chapter and also the book will have served their purpose if they help to stimulate reflection and debate.

References

Aranda S (2001) Silent voices hidden practices: exploring undiscovered aspects of cancer nursing. *Int J Palliat Nurs* **7**(44): 178–85

Barnes K (2001) Staff stress in the children's hospice: causes, effects and coping strategies. *Int J Palliative Nurs* **7**(5): 248–54

Borrell CS (1996) *Mental Health of the Workforce of NHS Trusts*. Final Report, Sheffield Institute of Work Psychology

Crouch D (2003) Combating stress. *Nursing Times* **99**(5): 22–5

Gill J (1995) Spiritual care of the terminally ill. *Community Nurse* March

Harding R (1996) Nurse stress in cancer and leukaemia care. *Paediatr Nurs* **8**(2): 24–7

Hicks MD, Lavender R (2001) Psychosocial practice trends in pediatric oncology. *J Pediatr Oncol Nurs* **18**(4): 143–53

McAliley LG, Lambert SA, Ashenberg MD, Dull SM (1996) Therapeutic relations decision making: the Rainbow Framework. *Pediatr Nurs* **22**(3): 199–203, 210

McSherry W (1996) Raising the spirits. *Nurs Times* **92**(3): 47–9

Morse MM (1991) Negotiating commitment and involvement in the nurse-patient relationship. *J Adv Nurs* **16**: 455–68

Nursing and Midwifery Council (2002) *Code of Professional Conduct*. NMC, London

Riches G, Dawson P (2000) *An Intimate Loneliness: Supporting bereaved parents and siblings* (Facing Death series: Clarke D, Series Ed). Open University Press, Buckingham: 15–48

Rushton CH, McEnhill M, Armstrong L (1996) Establishing therapeutic boundaries as patient advocates. *Pediatr Nurs* **22**(3): 185–9

Spinetta JJ, Jankovic M, Ben Arush MW *et al* (2000) Guidelines for the recognition, prevention and remediation of burnout in health care professionals participating in the care of children with cancer: Report of the SIOP working committee on psychosocial issues in pediatric oncology. *Med Pediatr Oncol* **35**: 122–5

Totya JP (1996) Exploring the boundaries of pediatric practice: nurse stories related to relationships. *Pediatr Nurs* **22**(3): 191–6

Vachon MLS (1998) Caring for the caregiver in oncology and palliative care. *Semin Oncol Nurs* **14**(2): 152–7

Williams A (2001) A literature review on the concept of intimacy in nursing. *J Adv Nurs* **33**(5): 660–7

Appendix 1: Useful contact numbers and wish foundations

Contact numbers

British Humanist Association
47 Theobalds Road, London, WC1 8SP
Tel: 020 7430 0908

Christian Lewis Children's Cancer Care
62 Walter Road, Swansea, SA1 4PT
Tel: 01792 480500

Childhood Cancer Helpline
Monday–Friday 10.00am–4.00pm
Freephone: 0800 303031

The Compassionate Friends
53 North Street, Bristol, BS3 1EN
Helpline: 0117 953 9639   Office: 0117 966 5202

CLIC-Sargent Cancer Care for Children
Griffen House, 161 Hammersmith Road, London, W6 8SG
Tel: 020 8752 2800

The Family Fund Trust
The Information Office, PO Box 50, York, YO1 9ZX
Tel: 01904 621115

Wish foundations

Children's Wish Foundation
117 George Street, London, W1H 7HF
Tel: 020 7324 9235   Fax: 020 7224 9236

Dreams Come True Charity Ltd
York House, Knockhundred Row, Midhurst, W. Sussex, B29 9DQ
Tel: 01730 815000   Fax: 01730 813141

Starlight Foundation
11–15 Emerald Street, London, WC1N 3QL
Tel: 020 7430 1642   Fax: 020 7430 1482

When You Wish Upon A Star
2nd Floor, Futurist House, Valley Road, Basford, Nottingham, NG5 1JE
Tel: 01159 791720   Fax: 01159 791720

Appendix 2: Financial support

Disability Living Allowance (DLA) is a benefit for children who have a serious illness or disability and require more help and care than other children of the same age. This help must have been needed for at least three months (the qualifying period), and is likely to be required for at least another six months. It is not means tested and is not subject to income tax. For children under the age of sixteen, the claim must be made on the child's behalf by the parent or guardian. Young people over the age of sixteen years may be eligible to claim DLA in their own right and should seek advice from their Sargent social worker or local benefits office.

Application for DLA is through completion of a detailed form, part of which has to be signed by someone who knows the child well, such as the doctor, paediatric oncology outreach nurse (POON) or Sargent social worker.

DLA comprises both a care component and a mobility component. The components have different rates, but are paid as a single benefit. The care component has lower, middle and higher rates, depending on the level of care required. The criteria are well documented in the paperwork provided, but cover the fact that the child has attention or supervision requirements substantially in excess of normal requirements for a child of that age (George *et al*, 2000). The mobility component has lower and higher rates. The child has to be aged five years or older to qualify for the lower rate, and three years or older for the higher rate. The claim can be made three months before the child reaches the relevant age, this counting as the qualifying period.

Invalid Care Allowance (ICA) is a means-tested benefit paid to people who are caring for someone who is severely disabled for thirty-five hours or more a week (George et al, 2000). Parents/ guardians receiving the middle or higher rates of DLA component, among other criteria, are eligible to apply. Parents/guardians are not eligible to apply if they are employed, receive an income over a certain level, or are in full-time education.

For families on a low income, a number of benefits are available, the two most important being Income Support and Working Families Tax Credit.

All benefits, apart from those received on account of DS1500, are reviewed regularly. Owing to the complexities of numbers and interactions of benefits available, it is recommended that families seek advice from their Sargent social worker before completing any forms.

Financial support for the family following the death of their child can also be provided. For families receiving DLA, the benefit stops on the date of death; for those receiving ICA the benefit continue for six weeks after the death.

Families may qualify for a funeral expenses payment if they satisfy certain criteria. A claim form, SF200, available from the hospital, funeral director or benefits office, sets out the eligibility criteria. Families on a low income may be eligible for financial support from a bereavement fund; enquiries should be made to the hospital. National or local charities may also be able to help, eg. Leukaemia Care may be able to help with money towards the cost of a headstone. It is strongly recommended that families seek advice from those familiar with these claims, such as a CLIC Sargent social worker.

January 2003

George C, Donnelly C *et al* (2000) Welfare Benefits Handbook 2000/2001. Child Poverty Action Group, London

Appendix 3: Taking controlled drugs abroad

To obtain a licence from the Home Office, the prescribing doctor should write to:

Action Against Drugs Unit
The Home Office
50 Queen Anne's Gate
London
SW1H 9AT
Tel: 020 7273 3806
Fax: 020 7273 2157

The following information should be included in the letter:

- Patient's full name, address and date of birth
- Country of destination
- Name, form, strength and total quantity of each controlled drug being taken out of the country
- Departure and return dates

The licence will only permit passage of drugs through customs in the UK; it has no legal status outside the UK. The embassy of the country being visited should be contacted to ascertain their regulations.

The maximum quantities of drugs that can be exported are:

- Morphine sulphate   1.2 g
- Diamorphine hydrochloride 1.35 g
- Methadone   500 mg
- Oxycodone   900 mg
- Codeine   no restrictions

Appendix 4: The West Midlands Paediatric Macmillan Team Bereavement Policy

◆ Families will be contacted within a week of the bereavement.

◆ Families will be notified of the bereavement policy.

◆ Families will continue to be contacted for two years following their bereavement. Some families will chose not to be contacted. This will be documented in their Macmillan notes.

◆ The level of contact for individual families will differ and is influenced by their unique circumstances. Contact should, however, be made at birthdays and anniversaries. This contact will be either by telephone, letter or face-to-face visit.

◆ The Macmillan strategy is to increase the interval between contacts over the two-year period, ie. more contact in year one.

◆ The Macmillan team will liaise with the Sargent team and other allied professionals to optimise bereavement support.

◆ If, after assessment during the two-year period, a Macmillan nurse feels that a family has complex bereavement needs, they will need to be referred to a specialist bereavement service.

◆ At the end of two years, any family still requesting bereavement support must be referred to a specialist service.

◆ Any Macmillan nurse having difficulties withdrawing from families must discuss the issues with the wider team.

Index

morphine 71, 74, 88, 99, 100
multicentre research ethics committee
    (MREC) 36
multidisciplinary team 4, 5, 9, 13, 56
multiprofessional team 156, 162
Muslims 136
mutual trust 42

N

nasogastric feeding 94, 96
nasogastric tubes 126, 140
nausea 72, 73, 76, 78, 79, 82, 88, 89, 90,
    92, 94, 95, 101
nebulised morphine 86
nerve compression 34
nerve damage 77, 78
neuroblastoma 29, 33, 83, 88, 92
neuropathic pain 77
noisy breathing ('death rattle') 88
non-opioid analgesia 70
non-steroidal anti-inflammatory drugs
    (NSAIDs) 28, 70, 78
non-verbal cues 44, 48
normality
  ~ maintaining 8
nutrition 120

O

occupational therapists 120, 121
ondansetron 95
open-door policy 6
open communication 42, 51
opioids 86, 91
  ~ alternative 78
  ~ side-effects of 76
opioid analgesia 61
oral analgesia 72
oral etoposide 31, 32, 33
organ donation 124
osteosarcoma 29
over-involved relationships 156, 157,
    159
oxycodone 78
oxygen concentrator 87

oxygen therapy 86

P

paediatric oncology community nurse 13
paediatric oncology model 12, 13
paediatric oncology nurse specialists 14
paediatric oncology outreach nurses
    group 68
paediatric oncology outreach nursing
    posts 7
paediatric palliative care
  ~ active treatment in 27
pain 28
  ~ atypical 80
  ~ management of 69, 70, 71, 72, 73,
    74, 75, 76, 77, 78, 79, 80, 81
  ~ non-pharmacological management
    of 80
  ~ pharmacological management of 69
palatability 31
palliation 2, 7, 9
palliative care
  ~ transition to 1
palliative chemotherapy 6, 7
palliative radiotherapy 27
palliative surgery 34
palliative therapy 1
pallor 83
pancytopenia 83
paracetamol 70, 84
parental adjustment 23
parental helplessness 23
parental protectiveness 134
partnership in care 15
pathological fractures 29
peer acceptance 140
penile erection 137
period pain 61
personal identity 135
phase II trials 37
phase I trials 36, 40
physical dependence 134
play therapists 28
play therapy 82
post-mortem 126, 127